FROM THE REPUBLIC OF CONSCIENCE

First published in 2009 by
Liberties Press
Guinness Enterprise Centre | Taylor's Lane | Dublin 8
www.libertiespress.com | info@libertiespress.com
+353 (1) 415 1287

Trade enquiries to CMD BookSource
55a Spruce Avenue | Stillorgan Industrial Park
Blackrock | County Dublin
tel: +353 (1) 294 2560 | Fax: +353 (1) 294 2564

Distributed in the United States by
Dufour Editions
PO Box 7 | Chester Springs | Pennsylvania | 19425

and in Australia by
James Bennett Pty Limited | InBooks
3 Narabang Way | Belrose NSW 2085

Liberties Press is a member of Clé,
the Irish Book Publishers' Association.

ISBN: 978 1905 483 73 0
2 4 6 8 10 9 7 5 3 1

A CIP record for this title is available from the British Library.

Typeset in Sabon by Sin É Design
Printed by Athenaeum Press

FROM THE REPUBLIC OF CONSCIENCE

Stories Inspired by the Universal Declaration of Human Rights

To the memory of Frank McCourt

Contents

Foreword

by Seán Love

This anthology developed from a conversation between myself and Roddy Doyle in late 2007. We were talking about the impending 60th anniversary of the Universal Declaration of Human Rights, as you do, and thought it would be interesting to illustrate each of the thirty Articles with a piece of creative writing – to try to show what they mean in the context of ordinary human life. So we decided to ask thirty Irish writers to choose an article each and create an imaginative response to it.

We wanted to ensure the stories would circulate as widely as possible, so we brought the idea to Gerry Smyth at the *Irish Times*. Gerry agreed to serialise the pieces on a weekly basis throughout 2008 and publish the full collection in magazine format on the actual anniversary, 10 December – including, with the assistance of Irish Aid, the distribution of one hundred thousand copies to Transition Year students across the island of Ireland.

We started approaching writers. We asked that each story or essay be quite brief, about one thousand, five hundred words in length. There was an immediate positive response, with thirty writers rapidly signing up. Inevitably, we did not even get to ask many other great writers. Of course, some Articles were in greater demand than others, but we managed to cover all thirty (thirty-one, even!) without falling-out with anyone. It is important to point out here that – in spite of Glenn Patterson's slanderous accusations of cronyism – while Roddy Doyle was first to sign up, he got last pick.

On 15 March, Seamus Heaney's introductory essay *The Poetic Redress*, alongside the 'verbal contraption' of his extraordinary poem 'From the Republic of Conscience', set the frame of reference for the series. Over the following months, all the writers faithfully delivered their stories/essays for the Saturday editions of the *Irish Times* – each approach ingeniously different from the preceding ones.

Most also read their stories at literary festivals and events during the course of the year, such as Listowel, Belfast, at the Electric Picnic and in Trinity College. At these readings, the discussions about how they had approached the task were always intriguing, sometimes inspiring and often hilarious.

Once the series had been completed, public interest suggested that publication of the anthology in book form would be an obvious next step. To further enhance the power of the collection, we asked twelve visual artists to respond to a story or essay of their choice. As with the writers, their goodwill was overwhelming. Louis le Brocquy agreed to provide the front cover, and each of the eleven other artists chose one of the stories from the collection. We asked for the artwork to be in black-and-white.

As you can see, the resulting collection is magnificent.

I want to thank all the writers and artists for their extraordinary generosity, and for giving their time, creativity and reputations to this project. I hope everyone will understand if I highlight one writer: not alone did Frank McCourt write a brilliant story, but last December 2008, at his own expense and in spite of health problems, he flew to Dublin to read his story along with the other writers in Trinity College, on International Human Rights Day. He brought the house down, as Alan Gilsenan's film of the night will confirm. I am so glad that I had the opportunity to send to Frank, in early May of this year, Nick Miller's remarkable artwork for his story. Frank loved it, describing it as 'nothing less than startling'.

I want to thank Gerry Smyth, Hugh Linehan and the *Irish Times* for their generosity, support and advice throughout this project. Thanks also to Irish Aid, who had the wisdom to sponsor the provision of several thousand copies of this book to secondary schools across the island. And finally, thanks to Liberties Press, who were the most creatively engaged of the publishers who approached us and have been a pleasure to work with.

Seán Love, commissioning editor of this volume, was Executive Director of Amnesty International, Ireland, from 2001 to 2008 and a founding director of Art for Amnesty and Amnesty Education. He has initiated several book projects for Amnesty, including the serial novel *Yeats is Dead* (Jonathan Cape, 2001) and the children's serial novel *Click* (Scholastic, 2007). He is currently Executive Director of Fighting Words creative writing centre in Dublin.

Introduction:
The Poetic Redress

by Seamus Heaney

In an essay published in 1998 to mark the fiftieth anniversary of
the Universal Declaration of Human Rights, Thomas
Buergenthal, a former President of the Inter-American Court of
Human Rights, drew an important distinction. He pointed out
that whereas the original Charter of the United Nations
internationalised human rights as a legal concept, the subsequent
Universal Declaration gave the concept moral force.

When the Declaration was being framed in 1948, several of
the UN member states were, for better or worse reasons, against
a document that would be legally binding, with the result that the
text is more akin to an exhortation than an edict. And yet, as
Buergenthal also pointed out, it is the 'eloquent, expansive and
simple' nature of the language in the document which has proved
most potent in the long run – as is evident from the brief First
Article:

> All human beings are born free and equal in dignity and rights. They are endowed with reason and conscience and should act towards one another in a spirit of brotherhood.

In the boldness and buoyancy of these words there are echoes of many of the great foundational texts of western civilisation, from Sophocles' 'wonders of man' chorus through Christ's Sermon on the Mount on up to the American Declaration of Independence and the French Declaration of the Rights of Man. So even if this First Article cannot guarantee what it declares, if its writ cannot be made to run in China or Zimbabwe or Guantánamo, it nevertheless gestures so confidently towards what human beings desire that it fortifies a conviction that the desirable can in fact be realised.

Over the past sixty years, of course, the philosophical basis of the Declaration in the western tradition has been contested, and increasingly so in the post-9/11 period, when a 'clash of civilisations' has been touted as the future way of the world. Even though the initial emphasis on 'brotherhood' is a reminder that the individual operates in a community, adversaries claim that the western concept is excessively individualistic and neglects community solidarity and cultural diversity. Yet it seems to me that this problematic truth can be acknowledged without relinquishing belief in the larger overall good which the Declaration has effected.

Since it was framed, the Declaration has succeeded in creating an international moral consensus. It is always there as a means of highlighting abuse if not always as a remedy: it exists instead in the moral imagination as an equivalent of the gold standard in the monetary system. The articulation of its tenets has made them into world currency of a negotiable sort. Even if its Articles are ignored or flouted – in many cases by governments who have signed up to them – it provides a worldwide amplification system for 'the still, small voice'.

Thus, Vaclav Havel can concede that in the decades since the Universal Declaration was adopted by the UN, human rights have been repeatedly violated or suppressed in many countries; yet he can also argue that these breaches of its principles have been far outweighed by the historic importance of the global covenant which it represents. It is, he says, 'an instrument holding up a mirror to the misery of the world'.

In that image, which echoes Hamlet's claim that plays and players 'hold, as 'twere, the mirror up to nature', we hear the voice of Havel the dramatist as much as the voice of Havel the former prisoner and victim of human rights abuse in a totalitarian system. We hear, in effect, the voice of the artist gaining on the voice of the activist, so it comes as no surprise to find him concluding that the roots of human rights lie deeper than the world of human covenants. They are far more profound than contracts between governments and have their origin in the metaphysical. How else, indeed, could the document enshrine words like 'dignity' and 'conscience', words that strain against the bonds of legal definition and political categorisation?

The thirty Articles of the Declaration, many of which are couched in a perfectly secular, civic idiom, do essentially rest upon this numinous, vestigially religious foundation. They were formulated at an opportune historical moment, by the representatives of peoples in shock at what had happened in the course of the Second World War, and ever since they have remained a force for historical good. Even in a world riven by fundamentalisms east and west, they persist as an audible, creditable and potentially credible strain.

Flouted though the Articles have been and continue to be, their vulnerability should perhaps be regarded as an earnest of their ultimate value. If, for example, an effort were to be made to enforce them by the exercise of military power – as in the effort to enforce 'democracy' on Iraq – it would not only end in failure but would discredit utterly the very concept of human rights. They would be stigmatised as the attributes of an imperium rather than an inherent endowment of the species.

It is this vulnerable yet spiritually inviolate quality which makes them attractive not only to the wronged and the oppressed of the earth, but to writers and poets as well. The Universal Declaration is not a sure-fire panacea for the world's ills; it is more geared to effect what I once called 'the redress of poetry' than to intervene like a superpower. This idea of redress I discovered first in Simone Weil's book *Gravity and Grace*, where she observes that if we know the way society is unbalanced, we must do what we can to add weight to the lighter side of the scale. The Universal Declaration, it seems to me, adds this kind of weight and contributes thereby to the maintenance of an equilibrium – never entirely achieved – between the rights and wrongs.

Writers and poets are also capable of adding this kind of weight, as is evident in this collection of responses to the Declaration. When faced with the direct speech of the Declaration, many of them sought to conjure up work that functions as a counterweight to the given actuality of the world. The writings they place in the scale may only be imagined, but if the imagining is credible, if it persuades us to suspend our disbelief, it will be part of the redress that human dignity, human rights, human reason, human consciousness all desire and deserve.

It is also a fact, however, that when it comes to creating work in support of a morally laudable cause or in response to an uplifting theme, writers and poets face a difficulty peculiar to their calling. They are not like speakers at a podium or preachers in a pulpit. Because of the artistic imperative they obey, they must do more than utter a commendable sentiment. They must make a thing of words, construct 'a verbal contraption'.

It is not enough for creative writers to be what Osip Mandelstam once called 'purveyors of the paraphrasable meaning', even if they happen to be paraphrasing the Universal Declaration; not enough merely to repeat what Joyce called 'the big words', even words like 'dignity' and 'conscience'; not enough to have the will doing the work of the imagination. Some kind of turn or twist or swerve, some shift in the mind or the medium has to occur, some little startle of insight or originality that may prompt the composition of a short lyric or the invention of an entire world – as in *Animal Farm*.

When, for example, the Polish poet Wislawa Szymborska contributed a poem entitled 'Tortures to Reflections on the Universal Declaration of Human Rights', a fiftieth-anniversary anthology which also included the essays of Havel and Buergenthal, she ended up by inverting a truth that has been regarded for millennia as self-evident. After four stanzas of relentless enumeration of the body's susceptibility to pain, of claims that nothing has changed, that in torture 'it still trembles as it trembled / before Rome was founded and after', that it still 'bruises, swells, drools and bleeds', Szymborska comes to the unexpected, heartbreaking conclusion that amid these landscapes of pain it is not the soul but the body which somehow proves everlasting:

The little soul roams among those landscapes,
disappears, returns, draws near, moves away,
evasive and a stranger to itself,
now sure, now uncertain of its own existence,
whereas the body is and is and is
and has nowhere to go.

The anthology (edited by Barend van der Heidjen and Bahia Tahzib-Lie, published by Kluwer Law International) also included 'From the Republic of Conscience', a poem I managed to write in 1985 when I was asked to contribute something to mark the year's United Nations Day. The request came from Mary Lawlor, the secretary of the local Sandymount branch of Amnesty International and now the Irish director of Front Line, the organisation which works for the protection of human rights defenders worldwide.

Mary's request was accompanied by a dossier containing the case histories of prisoners of conscience who had suffered everything from censorship and harassment to incarceration and torture, so I had a strong desire to come up with something good enough for the pamphlet Amnesty intended to publish. But I could find no way to invent 'a verbal contraption' that would be anywhere near as strong as the record of injustice and pain in those resolutely unpoetic press releases, and after a couple of weeks I wrote back to say I was unable to deliver.

But this removal of the sense of obligation shortened the creative odds: once the weight of the commission lifted, conditions were less earnest, less duty bound. Anxiety about measuring up to the grim evidence disappeared, replaced by a mood that was both apt and absolved, more susceptible to the spirit of play. Almost immediately I thought of an exercise I had set my writing students in Harvard the previous semester. I had asked them to imagine and describe a country that might stand as an allegory for some emotion or state of mind, so I now set myself the same exercise; make up a country called 'Conscience'.

I took it that Conscience would be a republic, a silent, solitary place where a person would find it hard to avoid self-awareness and self-examination; and this made me think of Orkney. I remembered the silence the first time I landed there. When I got off the small propeller plane and started walking across the grass to a little arrivals hut, I heard the cry of a curlew. And as soon as that image came to me, I was up and away, able to proceed with a fiction that felt workable yet unconstrained, a made-up thing that might be hung in the scale as a counterweight to the given actuality of the world.

From the Republic of Conscience

by Seamus Heaney

I

When I landed in the republic of conscience
it was so noiseless when the engines stopped
I could hear a curlew high above the runway.

At immigration the clerk was an old man
who produced a wallet from his homespun coat
and showed me a photograph of my grandfather.

The woman in customs asked me to declare
the words of our traditional cures and charms
to heal dumbness and avert the evil eye.

No porter. No interpreter. No taxi.
You carried what you had to and very soon
your symptoms of creeping privilege disappeared.

II

Fog is a dreaded omen there but lightning
spells universal good and parents hang
swaddled infants in trees during thunderstorms.

Salt is their precious mineral. And seashells
are held to the ear during births and funerals.
The base of all inks and pigments is seawater.

Their sacred symbol is a stylized boat.
The sail is an ear, the mast a sloping pen,
the hull a mouth-shape, the keel an open eye.

At their inauguration, public leaders
must swear to uphold unwritten law and weep
to atone for their presumption to hold office –

and to affirm their faith that all life sprang
from salt in tears which the sky-god wept
after he dreamt his solitude was endless.

III

I came back from that frugal republic
with my two arms the one length, the customs woman
having insisted my allowance was myself.

The old man rose and gazed into my face
and said that was official recognition
that I was now a dual citizen.

He therefore desired me when I got home
to consider myself a representative
and to speak on their behalf in my own tongue.

Their embassies, he said, were everywhere
but operated independently
and no ambassador would ever be relieved.

PAGES FROM AN ALIEN DICTIONARY

by Joseph O'Connor

ARTICLE 1

All human beings are born free
and equal in dignity and rights.
They are endowed with reason
and conscience and should act
towards one another in a
spirit of brotherhood.

Tryst (the Earthly Garden), 2009, charcoal on paper, Alice Maher, photo taken by Michael McLoughlin

LOVE: Noun used among the earthlings; also verb, form of address, term of affection among them; frequent subject of primitive attempts at literary or artistic expression by their poets, bards, etc.

Definition(s):

The opposite of hate (James Joyce);

The same old thing that made the preacher lay the Bible down (Muddy Waters);

The realisation that another person is real (Iris Murdoch);

The force that through the green fuse drives the flower (Dylan Thomas – inebriate of the subspecies 'Welsh', endangered);

What can happen in a time of cholera (Gabriel García Márquez);

All you need (The Beatles);

The thing I can't buy (The Beatles);

The thing for sale (Billie Holiday);

The greatest of these (St Paul to the Corinthians);

The thing that is lovelier the second time around (St Francis Sinatra);

The thing that is tainted (Marc Almond and Soft Cell);

The thing in which we are enfolded (Julian of Norwich);

The thing I am in – ooh-bee-doo – with Den-eeh (Deborah Harry and Blondie).

The indigenous, known as humans, a weak and childish life form, profess these most blatantly nonsensical unrealities, going so far as to avow themselves, in pitiable manner, possessed of certain inalienable advantages, for which no word exists in our beautiful language, but which they, in their selection of grunts, call 'rights'.

These they have organised into a charter, or statement, to which little attention is paid by the less snivelling of their rulers. This nodule of delusion, in their principal tongue (an ugly patois best suited to evading true communication) amuses by stating the following outrages: 'All human beings are born free and equal in dignity and rights. They are endowed with reason and conscience and should act towards one another in a spirit of brotherhood.' Yet remarkably, the great majority, while avowing the importance of these absurdities, have privately more complicated responses to the proposal of brotherhood. The following is a selection of transcribed material, recorded recently by our advance party of operatives in [name of Earth-country deleted]:

> . . . I don't like yer man. I can't stick yer woman. Don't ask me about that crowd because you'll only get me going. Look at the hairdo. Look at the walk of it. I'd say she says more than her prayers, wouldn't you? Course you know about him. Did you never hear that? Sure, that's well known. That's gospel fact. They're ignorant, they are. It's the way they were raised. Course I'm tolerant to the last. Don't care where anyone's from. They're equal in my book. Give everyone a break. I'm big into that. I was anti-apartheid. My cleaning lady is Chinese. I can't abide intolerance. I don't do prejudice. But you know what they're like. They can't help it, God love them, it's in their DNA. Not that I've anything against them.
>
> They stick to their own. Oh, thicker than thieves. Don't want to know the rest of us. Don't want to mix in. Think they're better than us. Their discos, their pubs. Equal rights they want now, if you don't mind, Missus. Their rights and their dignity and the front of the queue,

and the hand in your face for whatever they can get, but you can say nothing these days, so I keep my opinion to myself, but between you and me, and a hole in the wall, I'd trust any living one of them as far as I could spit a rat. Not that I'm prejudiced mind you.

Oh, yes. I say nothing. But I watch. And I learn. I knew one of them once. No I'm serious. And I made the effort. Tried to make conversation. Went down to her level but do you think I got thanks? But see, what can you do? You're irrelevant these days. You're normal, you're nothing. And you cannot get through to them. Banging your head off that wall, so you are. World of their own. Away with the fairies. They're not the same, I'm sorry, but it has to be said. Even the way they look at you, the way they go on. They think scruples is a nightclub. Think ethics is in England. Think the ten bloody commandments is a mountain range some place. Think the law is an ass. And they laugh at us, you know. Oh they are scuttering themselves laughing. And why wouldn't they laugh, says you? They're on the pig's back. They have friends in high places. The *Irish Times* is full of them. So is RTÉ. Sure that's well known. Did you never hear that? If Fintan O'Toole isn't one of them, he'd help them out if they were stuck. As for Tubridy – ah, I better not start.

But you can say nothing these days. You're branded if you do. It's political correctness gone bats, so it is. Can't have a joke. Can't have a good laugh. You're suddenly a bigot. Can't open your beak. It's the thought police I'm telling you. Orwell was right. Give them an inch and they'll take the whole mile. Next thing you know they're up on their back legs and yapping about their rights and their this and their that. If anything I'm too tolerant. Really I am. I take everyone at face value. I'm gullible. But you have to draw the line. I mean, really and truly, would you want any child of yours to marry one of them, being honest? I don't mean to be prejudiced. Ask anyone, they'll tell you. It's each to their own and hail fellow well met and the benefit of the doubt and whatever you're having yourself. But who in the name of Jesus do they think they are? What are they on? What are they like? Why are they trying to shove it down our throats? Why can't they keep to themselves?

They've one of them working in the Spar up above. I see him every day. Every day! Not one of the nice humble type, not grateful or anything. But bold as brass. The look in his eye. It's like: 'I'm here. And I want my rights.' But I don't like to say anything. Well these days you can't. Open your gob and come out with a joke and you'd swear you'd invented Guantánamo Bay or lurried your granny into Abu Ghraib to be waterboarded. They're organised, you see. You wouldn't be up to them. Want to change our way of life. And we'd want to wise up. You mark my words. We'll be sorry before we're finished. There's one of them next door to you. And they're talking to your kids. Pumping them full of nonsense. Propaganda. It's everywhere. Schools, universities. The box, the radio. They've Newstalk infested, and Gerry Ryan, and TV3. Vincent Browne is in their pay and so's the half of Dáil Éireann, and Senator David bloody Norris is their secret commander, and just you wait and see if it doesn't come true. I may not be perfect. I'm not claiming that. But you go to bloody war with the army you've got. I'm all for

people's rights. Give me a petition, I'll sign it. But Jesus,
it has to stop somewhere . . .

Thus, the earthlings, while professing adherence and obedience
to 'love', find a kind of inter-binding, and a solace from their pain,
by generating noises such as those transcribed above, and other
derisive emissions. And yet, as has been noted by the Ministry of
Research, they fail to find the courage to live in freedom from
love's tyranny. In private, they long for it, believing it makes them
better, and their daubers and scribblers, as well as their children,
are so obsessed with it as to make one pity the whole life form on
this lonely and desolate star. So far from their excellence, they look
up at the night, clinging often to their words and their sounds for
consolation, and to the tiniest hope that they are somehow not
alone on their rock as it glides through the nothing.

See:

'We must love one another or die' (W. H. Auden) (They must
love one another and die, in truth);

'Love ceases to be a pleasure, when it ceases to be a secret'
(Aphra Behn);

'Tis better to have loved and lost than never to have loved'
(Alfred Tennyson);

'All that matters is love and work' (Sigmund Freud);

'Love's pleasure lasts but a moment; love's sorrow lasts all
through life' (Jean-Pierre de Florian);

'How strange, the change from major to minor, every time
we say goodbye' (Cole Porter);

'Every man is a poet when he is in love' (Plato);

'If I am pressed to say why I loved him, I feel it can only be
explained by replying: "Because it was he, because it was
me"'(Montaigne);

'Many waters cannot quench love; neither can the floods drown it' (Song of Solomon);

'Two things a man cannot hide: that he is drunk, and that he is in love' (Antiphanes);

'Love does not consist in gazing at each other, but in looking outward in the same direction' (Antoine de Saint-Exupéry);

'You can't live without it – take a tip from one who's tried' (Robert Dylan, primitive melodist, one of their bards);

'You have never been in love until you've watched the dawn rise on the Home for the Blind' (Dr Stephen P. Morrissey, perhaps the strangest of their species);

'There's nothing half so sweet in life as love's young dream' (Thomas Moore);

'Men have died from time to time and worms have eaten them, but not for love' (William Shakespeare);

'My love's a noble madness' (John Dryden, a 'poet');

'Love has pitched his mansion in the place of excrement' (William Yeats);

'Don't know much about history / Don't know much biology / But I do know that I love you, / and I know that if you loved me too, / what a wonderful world this would be' (Sam Cooke, profession unknown, evidently not historian or biologist.)

Thus, 'love' appears frequently in manifestly untrue and infantile statements, which are nonetheless widely believed and circulated among the earthlings. Take note: No translation into our language is possible for this term. Its use among the Secret Invasion Force (SIF), already in place on Earth and awaiting further orders, has been sternly discouraged by High Military Command, as has the offensive term 'human rights'. Humans do not have rights. They were born to be slaves. These usages by the native earthlings are to be forcibly discontinued, by selective employment of torture if necessary, as soon as full colonisation of their planet is effected. Let loose the droids of war.

ON BEING ASKED TO WRITE 1,500 WORDS TO CELEBRATE THE UNIVERSAL DECLARATION OF HUMAN RIGHTS

by Neil Jordan

ARTICLE 2

Everyone is entitled to all the rights and freedoms set forth in this Declaration, without distinction of any kind, such as race, colour, sex, language, religion, political or other opinion, on the basis of the political, jurisdictional or international status of the country or territory to which a person belongs, whether it be independent, trust, non-self-governing or under any other limitation of sovereignty.

Amelia Stein

I was asked by the Amnesty man to write a piece to celebrate the anniversary of the Universal Declaration of Human Rights. I agreed, immediately, because not to agree would seem churlish, and would typecast me as the 'kind of person who doesn't do this kind of thing'. In a romantic comedy, someone who smokes and steps on the tails of pets is not the kind of person who you want to get the girl in the end. Neither, probably, is someone who doesn't want to write 1,500 words to celebrate the anniversary of the Universal Declaration of Human Rights. So I naturally said yes. But the first problem was, I had never read the Universal Declaration of Human Rights.

The only acquaintance I had with the document was when it was projected on a large screen at a U2 concert in Toronto. The idea of projecting the Universal Declaration of Human Rights to a group of 80,000 people who had probably never read it either was a good one, but the idea of making them pay for the privilege bordered on genius. It was a far better idea than Tom Sawyer's one of getting his friends to pay for the privilege of painting his auntie's fence. Tom Sawyer was paid in apple cores and lollipop sticks and rusty bolts and things, but those concert-goers in Toronto didn't pay with apple cores, they paid with serious money, around $100 a ticket.

Anyway, I was so overwhelmed by the brilliance of the idea that I didn't pay any attention to the specific articles in the Universal Declaration of Human Rights, so now, several years later, I turned on my computer, downloaded the document for free and read it properly. Each of the articles seemed admirable, in their intent and their definition of what rights a person on this planet should have, but the immediate problem was that most of them were taken, by other writers who had been asked to write their 1,500 words on the Universal Declaration of Human

Rights. I had met a very nice and troubled man once who had been tortured in an Iranian prison and thought I might write about that, but was told that Article 5 was taken, so Roddy Doyle or Colm Tóibín or Anne Enright or some other writer would be writing about torture, which excluded me. Damn.

I then thought I could write about Article 9, which states 'No one shall be subjected to arbitrary arrest, detention or exile', and called up to say I would write about that, but was told that Tom Humphries was writing about Article 9. I did not know Tom Humphries as a writer, then remembered he was the guy who wrote colourful articles about sport for the *Irish Times* and thought, good luck to him, he would probably write a good article about arbitrary arrest, imprisonment and exile.

In fact, Articles 1, 3, 4, 5, 6, 9, 12, 15, 18, 23, 24, 25, 26 were all taken. All that remained to me were the less interesting articles, about the rights to social security and participation in government directly or through freely chosen representatives. So I settled on Article 2, which reads: 'Everyone is entitled to all the rights and freedoms set forth in this Declaration, without distinction of any kind, such as race, colour, sex, language, religion, political or other opinion, national or social origin, property, birth or status. Furthermore, no distinction shall be made on the basis of the political, jurisdictional or international status of the country or territory to which the person belongs, whether it be independent, trust, non-self-governing or any other limitations of sovereignty.'

It wasn't great, but it was one of the only ones left. It seemed to say that the entire declaration applies to everyone, regardless of etc. The basic proposition, that the Articles should apply to all of us who match the definition human, seemed good, true and unarguable. But my problems then multiplied. What could

I write about a proposition that seemed so self-evident? A piece of fiction, perhaps, about a being to whom it should, but didn't, apply? A benign and maybe well-intentioned alien who had in all innocence travelled across the wastes of space and time to our beautiful planet, that was having its inner organs examined by NASA types? I could picture its eyes like reflective saucers and its mouth, in the shape of a red cross, saying NGYLOUP-PRUDDER, which when translated means, please get them to stop doing that.

But then such a piece of fiction would itself seem churlish, against the spirit of the project, and somebody who wrote that would have even less chance of getting the girl in the romantic comedy. I was getting depressed. I began to wonder was it possible that a simple request to write 1,500 words about the Universal Declaration of Human Rights and their inability to do it could induce a spiritual crisis in a person, leading to depression, suicide or even random murder, much the way Heinrich von Kleist realised the pointlessness of life by studying a Romanesque arch and realising it was only held in place by its instinct to collapse, and subsequently killed himself. Kleist's unique insight, the austere brilliance of it and the bald, brutal courage of the outcome, both seemed beyond me at this point. And I got further depressed, realising that I was the kind of person who doesn't even have the courage to top himself because he can't write the required 1,500 words. Then I thought, maybe I'll write a romantic comedy about a man trying to win the love, admiration and respect of a girl by writing 1,500 words about the Universal Declaration of Human Rights. I didn't know how it would begin, how it would develop, how all those delightful confusions, red herrings and blind alleys are transformed etc, but I had a very clear idea as to how it should end . . .

EXT. CAFÉ. BOULEVARD DES CAPUCHINS. EVENING.
Evening, because we can have that beautifully pearly light that is
appropriate to the emotion we want to invoke, which is misty-
eyed, tearful, but also reassures us that we have not spent the last
two hours in vain, instead have ingested, while being teased,
amused, delighted, moved, a cunningly disguised moral lesson.
He, smoking a cigarette, squishing it beneath his white trainers
(he wears trainers, but with a rather elegant pinstriped overcoat
dangling right to the edge of his turned-up jeans, the kind of
couture that Mick Jagger wore when he accepted his knighthood)
and opens the glass café door.

INT. CAFÉ. BOULEVARD DES CAPUCHINS. EVENING.
A cat squeals. That furred thing by the carpet was its tail.
Damn. Anyway, he walks through the cosmopolitan crowd to
get a view of–

JUSTINE.
She has a scarf wrapped round her neck, wearing one of those
negligee bustier things over a pair of jeans. (You know the time
when underwear became outerwear and you weren't supposed
to comment on it, but something seismic had changed? Anyway
. . .) Justine is beautiful, of course, she is an intern with the UN,
has worked in the past for Médecins Sans Frontières and helped
arrange Madonna's adoption. Anyway, she is very desirable, has a
very large flat overlooking the etc. And she is reading two typed
pages, 1,500 words, to be exact.

He comes behind her. But she doesn't raise her head. She is so
absorbed. He touches her cheek.

She absently nibbles at his forefinger. Then takes a drag from
the lighted cigarette by the ashtray. (She can smoke even though

he can't, something to do with our foreknowledge of the fact that she'll give it up the minute she finds out she's pregnant. That is, if she keeps the baby, which in a romantic comedy she has to — if she doesn't keep it, it becomes what a friend of mine used to call a 'searing indictment', in other words, a movie about the real world and its issues.)

Anyway, she absently nibbles at his forefinger.

BERNARD (his name) What do you think?

JUSTINE It's good, it's good . . . maybe even better than good . . . Let me finish . . .

And then I thought, no, you can't conclude a romantic comedy with the girl nibbling at the guy's forefinger. She has to be running through an airport, or leaping at the last possible moment through the sliding doors of a subway into his arms, the pages containing the 1,500 words about Article 2 of the Universal Declaration of Human Rights blowing around them like leaves or confetti, she apologising, scrambling to pick them up while concluding that interrupted kiss, forefingers and nibblings have nothing to do with the business of romantic comedies, nor with the business of the anniversary of the Universal Declaration of Human Rights. It is time to get serious here. And I took out the Declaration again and re-read Article 2: 'Everyone is entitled to all the rights and freedoms set forth in this declaration, without distinction of any kind, such as race, colour, sex, language, religion, political or other opinion, national or social origin, property, birth or other status.

'Furthermore, no distinction shall be made on the basis of the political, jurisdictional or international status of the country or territory to which a person belongs, whether it be independent, trust, non-self-governing or under any other limitation of sovereignty.'

And I remembered a quote, something I had recently read, which illuminated the problem. It wasn't that the proposition was self-evident. It was something else entirely.

Tertullian, a Carthaginian theologian, around 200 AD, on Christianity: *Certum est, quia impossible*. Because it is impossible, it must be true.

THE SMELL OF ROSES

by Dermot Healy

ARTICLE 3

Everyone has the right to life,
liberty and security of person.

The day we arrived in Ecuador we spoke in Irish. Through a timber worker en route to Colombia we found a room in a hotel. All we had with us was a letter of introduction to the cultural aide, the phone numbers of the Irish Consul, and a Divine Word missionary. At breakfast, the waitress lit a Carroll I gave her, and threw marvelling eyes at the ceiling. We took our first walk in Quito, stepping downstairs into memory.

The street was filled with the smell of fireworks from a festival of the night before.

I dropped a dollar into the cap of a man. He was sitting, head down, on a deckchair on the street, with one hand palm-upwards. He had enormous blue-veined thighs wrapped in bandages, and huge crutches.

His fingers wriggled in reply.

I met him again a few days later in a park, where we went to watch three-man-a-side netball. He was lying back, eyes closed, with his legs crossed, hidden in a copse of trees. Then we encountered him being dropped off at five in the morning onto his patch. Two helpers were wrapping the bloody bandages round his thigh, and painting the blue sores onto his skin, for the day ahead.

When he saw me he rose a finger to his lips. I dropped a dollar at his feet. He gave a grand gesture. I winked at him and he stared back outraged. The wink, I later learned, means that you are about to inform on someone.

We got an apartment after two days. Each morning Indians on the street below opened rubbish bags, took what they needed, and retied the bags. The poor dressed in white. McDonald's had armed personnel on the door. The Indians studied us as we set off each morning to various government buildings with the letter of introduction, but each time we arrived to the wrong door. A woman on the street felt my beard. We ate in a local café, and I led the way home. We were walking in a breathless maze for forty-five minutes.

'Are you sure you know the way?'

'Yes.'

'How do you know?'

'I took down the name of the street.'

'What is it?'

'Una Via,' I said.

'One way,' she said. I had brought us back up through all the one-way streets in Quito.

On another aimless walk, I tried a police station. I was searched and shown upstairs to see the chief. It was 4.30 of a Friday. He was sitting alone in an office laughing to himself. I gave him the letter and he offered me a rum. Two men materialised alongside the far wall.

'You seek Senior Philatao?'

'Yes.'

He laughed, lifted up the phone and rang, and shook his head. 'Go to the Casa Cultura,' he said.

We went to the museum the next day, and for the first time got out of the modern city into the old. We began to feel more at home, as our estrangement grew, but found no cultural aide. We stood outside. The army passed, rifles cocked. I looked up at a sculpture of a boy archer on the balcony of the building.

'Do you see him,' I asked. 'See how he is shooting the arrow out.'

'He is shooting it in.'

'Out,' I said.

'In,' she said. 'Everything I say or do, you find fault with,' and she burst into tears. A small angel had started a row between us.

The smell of fireworks was at its height. We climbed back to the apartment exhausted. The night grew dark. I phoned the Irish Consul. It rang out. We watched a lady cook on the TV. Her hair went into the soup.

'What's going on?'

'I don't know.'

I lifted out the phone number of the Divine Word missionary that a philosopher I hardly knew had given me in the bar of the Abbey Theatre. I rang, and a voice answered in Spanish.

'Do you speak English?' I asked.

'Are you Irish?'

'Yes, and there's something wrong.'

'Where are you?' he asked, and in ten minutes he climbed up the stairs, entered the living room and looked at us and said: 'You have altitude sickness, you are at 11,500 feet.'

A weight lifted off my head.

Through him we would visit the equator; and join a protest march in solidarity when six priests, and their housekeeper, were killed in San Salvador. The brains of the religious were cut out. Priests in shawls arrived from all the poor quarters. A nun grabbed the mike outside the university and said she was ashamed to teach among Jesuits who had let the deaths pass without protest.

At the Peruvian border, we would attend a mass for the second funeral of a woman who was dug up a year after she died because a voice told her son she was in the wrong grave. We'd visit the Village of White Fools. We tried to visit the Virgin on the heights of Quito, but the woman in the shop at the bottom of the steep ascent said, 'No Señor,' when I told her where we were going.

She stood in front of us on the road, looked at Helen, and

drew her hand across her throat. We turned back. She had saved us from knife-wielding toughs above at the monument. We found the cultural aide, an office and a translator. With the oxygen reaching our brains, we moved into a hotel room in the old town, and planned trips to the Valley of the Volcanoes. I met an American historian who taught us how Magic Realism came out of the forests. When the woods were cut down, like in North America, the magic was lost.

I was coming home from my first day at my desk on a bus. To my right, on the street outside, there was uproar. Suddenly a soldier fired off a round of tear gas that landed in through the door. Everyone jumped out, including the driver. Crowds ran. I ducked with a man into a courtyard. We put our heads into a fountain, lifted our mouths to breathe but the arcade had a roof, and the place was filling up with bitter smoke.

We were collapsing with coughing, and tears, when a small door opened and a prostitute ushered the two of us into two indoor toilets. We stood silently alone. She let us out when the danger had passed. We walked down the hill with handkerchiefs to our faces, and shook hands outside the hotel.

The fireworks were tear gas; the festivals confrontations between student activists and soldiers. The workers supported the students, but paid for it. Buses were banned. Each late afternoon I joined the workers trudging home. Outside the hotel, another confrontation started. A woman and her children got caught in the swirls of gas. Helen lifted one kid and ran along with the mother up a hill and hid in a church.

Inside, Christ wore a Panama hat.

When we came out, the women were waving rolled lumps of lit newspapers to clear the pepper from the air. Next morning on my way to work I arrived into a stand-off. The students, in a side alley, were facing police and soldiers out on the main street. I looked round the corner judging the run. One policeman raised his hand, a student answered in reply, all weapons were lowered, and they let me cross.

We were invited to a concert. My translator showed us into seats in a private box. At the end of the show the lover was dancing to a lament as her man played the guitar to the side. Suddenly, rose petals, in thousands, fell down onto her, and into the gods. The roses stopped, then the skies opened again, and it began to rain; and underneath, the singer stood drenched in a garden of petals.

I found a distant other sense awakening. The applause started. The rain stopped. Helen's hand came down on mine. It was as if we had stepped out into the open air, as slowly, the waft of roses, at last, reached us in the balcony.

The audience came to their feet.

It was the most powerful, yet faint, sensation of smell I have ever experienced.

We tiptoed round in circles down the winding stairs and out onto the street. A few minutes later a jeep pulled in, braked hard, and two armed policemen jumped out with batons. They grabbed two lads who were walking ahead of us, and began hauling them across the foot path.

Suddenly Helen ran up, and touched one of the policemen lightly on the shoulder and shouted 'Theatre!'

He swung round.

'Señora?'

'Theatre!' She pointed back at the concert hall; and the lads, who looked like trainee clerics, began nodding. 'They were at the theatre.'

'Theatre?' asked the policeman.

'Sí,' said Helen.

'Sí, Sí,' said the lads.

We showed him our passports. The police got into the van and drove away.

'Gracias Señora, gracias,' said the students.

They were shaking. One lad drew the third of a Carroll into his lungs. We walked a little way along together, then we stopped, and reluctantly they went on, but kept looking back at us, waving.

A few weeks later on Stephen's Day our boat broke down on a tributary of the Amazon miles away from everyone. The boatman handed me the rope. I pulled hard, the engine took, and then gave again; we tied up, and set off afraid into the isolated jungle in search of someone the boatman knew. He began shouting a name into the trees. 'Marcos!' 'Marcos!' As darkness fell, a voice answered. That night we slept in a hammock in a small wooden hut in the forest. In through the canes next morning came a far away scent that we knew of old.

LOST IN ARIZONA

by Zlata Filipović

ARTICLE 4

No one shall be held in slavery
or servitude; slavery and the
slave trade shall be prohibited
in all their forms.

All she wants is to go for a cup of coffee . . .

She looks at me. Measures up me and the other girl who came in with me today, both of us clutching our note pads, full of questions. We came to learn from her, she is a living example both of us are writing our theses about. I am here to get more of the political-social perspective, while Maya (we met on the stairs, just before entering the room) is doing her thesis on the psychological effects. Maya is the only one writing about this topic, and I can tell she is excited at the prospect of getting the position of an assistant to the main professor, all going well, fingers crossed.

Barbara keeps looking at us, while Alma, her 'guardian', is explaining more about how she came to know Barbara. Rather, how Barbara ended up knowing Alma. Barbara is looking down at her hands which she crossed on her lap. She occasionally raises her eyes to look at me and Maya, while we frantically take notes. She cuts through Alma's delivery of facts and looks me straight in the eyes, then drops them to my feet and in broken language she says, 'I like your sandals'. I am confused, I didn't expect her to speak – to speak my language, or speak at all. Of course she would, she has been in my country for many years now. She chews her gum, sports cropped hair – that short, practical hairstyle women sometimes get in their forties and carry for the rest of their lives. It clashes with her young face, she is only nineteen. I notice her skin, beautiful, porcelain-like, and her heart-shaped face. Small blue eyes look straight into mine, she looks at me tough, provocatively. I feel she wants to show she is fine, she can manage, she will be fine. She looks both at me and the psychology MPhil student as though we are little girls, even though we are a few years older than her. There are questions in her eyes asking why are we here, what do we want. She then looks out the window, into the sunny day. The length of her gaze at the sunny town underneath screams of her desire to be outside.

I know Maya and I have both read everything there is to read on her and so many other girls, young women who ended up living her story. We have the non-governmental organisation reports, their statistics, country profiles, testimonies, legal documents, some psychological assessments. Barbara is the final link in the chain of completing our research. Then we can write it all up and submit, maybe even get a distinction.

I look at Barbara's hands. She bites her fingernails, but still has remnants of purple nail varnish close to the nail roots. There are round, light-brown marks – scars scattered along her forearms. It looks like the round marks of vaccinations we get as children. Looking at them today, we have forgotten how we screamed and cried the day we got them. But these marks are different, I have read about them – these are cigarette burns. She wears a sleeveless top, tight denim shorts, and platform mules. She doesn't mind her scars are showing.

Alma continues talking about the work of the organisation, the difficulty with funding, when Barbara jumps through Alma's words again – 'You want to know what happened? That is why you are here, right? My grandmother sold me. Some men came into the village, offered a big wad of euros which she quickly took into her old, dirty hands. She said she needed the money to educate my younger brother, make something useful of him. She has been taking care of my brother and I ever since our mother left. No one knows where my mother is, I have gotten used to the fact I have no mother. Grandmother was never kind, she beat me and made me work in the house and the garden. She was glad to get rid of me, and the witch even got some money in return. And boys are always better, girls don't bring anything but trouble. She saw that with her own daughter, my mother I never knew.

'The men said I will go to Germany to work in a family as a cleaner, and they packed me and four other girls into a big van and we drove for hours, days. We had no light in there, we heard lots of different languages spoken outside of the truck, stopping every so often. They let us out twice to go to the toilet and gave us some bread. Next time I saw light I was in front of 'Arizona'. They spoke in a language similar to mine, so I understood a bit. I realised 'Arizona' was not Germany. I knew there was no family for me to work in. They packed us girls into this club – that is what 'Arizona' was. The man who looked like some boss gave us dresses and high heels and said we were lucky because we could now work and pay back the money our families got, otherwise they didn't know what they might have to do to our families. One of the girls started crying, she had a baby back home. I didn't care what happened to the old witch, but I love my little brother and didn't want anything bad to happen to him. The men said it cost them a lot to bring us here, to give us this chance. We first needed to pay back our transport and visas, and then we would pay back the money our families got. Then we would start getting something for ourselves. We had to do what they told us, but it could all be over soon, as soon as we earned back the money. So I worked, you know?'

Maya and I are no longer taking notes.

'Men kept coming in, drunken, fat, angry. They told me you had a war in this country. I don't understand, what is wrong with you people? All these men coming in to 'Arizona' were former soldiers, policemen – mad – they had to get what they wanted. Each one had a gun or a knife in their pockets, some came in their uniforms. We had to dance and when they wanted to be with us, we had to go. I didn't like the music, it was loud and had these strong beats. I like nice stuff, like this Irish band, The Corrs. I like this song 'Dreams', you know it?

'Sometimes, there were twelve, fifteen of them in one night. I had a boyfriend back home, he was from my town so I had already done it before. But these men asked for strange things, and if I didn't give them what they wanted, they beat me, put cigarettes into my skin, played with a knife on my body. They said I am a whore. I didn't listen, I wasn't there. I learnt this trick of not feeling like I was in the room with them.

'We slept during the day in a room with lots of beds, and then had to get dressed up, put on make-up and go on the dancefloor again. Night into night, week into week. How long was I there, Alma?'

Alma responds: 'Two and a half years.'

'Yeah, so . . . There was a big lock on the door of the dormitory, and big men who stood on the door of the club. You couldn't go outside.

'I became friends with Lena, she was also sixteen, she was in the club before me. Our beds were near, so sometimes we did each other's make-up. Sometimes Lena cried and I stroked her hair like a little baby's, like my brother's. The owner of the club gave Lena some white pills one night, and Lena didn't remember what happened. She didn't know how to do the trick of not feeling like she was there. She liked not remembering, so took another pill, and one every night. She started shaking during the day, sleeping all day until I would have to get her out of bed, do her make-up, and then she'd have another pill. She stopped crying, just slept and waited for the next time she could have the little white pill. She really wasn't there, it wasn't like my trick. After one night she didn't come back to dormitory, I asked where she was. The boss slapped me hard, my nose spurted blood, it was like a bloody tap. I kept telling Lena one day we would be out, and go for coffee together and go shopping with the money we will get from all this. But after that time the boss hit me, I never saw or mentioned Lena again.'

Barbara now sleeps again in another dormitory, with lots of other girls like her. They don't speak to each other. Local volunteer women come in and make them knit and draw, and talk. 'It is so boring, what do I need to knit for?' It is called a 'safe house', there is a big sign outside that says 'Woman 21'. Alma's son comes sometimes, he teaches computers. He is nice, has nice hands with long fingers when he types on the computer. He is the only man apart from the lawyer who comes in. They are trying to organise something with the courts, but Barbara doesn't want to go. 'What do I need to go to court for? They are all the same anyway, I remember hearing the judge was sometimes coming into the club. And policemen – the same ones who said they will kill me. What do I get by going to court for?'

'Do you want to go home?' speaks Maya, for the first time.

Barbara is imprisoned even though she is now safe – she has no status, no documents. She knows too much about the dark side of this town. She has seen fathers, brothers, policemen, businessmen, judges who came to the club, they went into the rooms with her. At home, she has no one but her grandmother, maybe still her brother.

She looks out through the sun-filled window again.

'Let's go for a cup of coffee.'

I JUST DON'T LIKE THE SCREAMING

by Colum McCann

ARTICLE 5

No one shall be subjected to
torture or to cruel, inhuman
or degrading treatment
or punishment.

In the east we've got the Water Machines. They produce a scream like none you've ever heard before. Today it's Raoul. He's brown as a dog. He is hauled first by the hair over the low wall. He wears no shirt. His body is scraped along the ribcage. He wears a little religious medal at his neck. He is barefoot. When he kicks his heels, the bottoms of his feet are white. I find that curious. How can someone be so dark but their palms and soles are so white? He shouts, Please no. We laugh. Please no.

The heat bears down on the tarmac. There are six of us. We like working the Water Machine on a day like today. It's the coolest place. We can allow the spray to dampen our faces. It feels like a soft wet cloth on our shirts. Raoul tries struggling to get free. They all do. I have no idea why they don't find out sooner or later that it's easier to accept it. They don't have to struggle, they should just take what's coming to them. It's easier that way. Then we can finish them off and just throw them over the wall to join all the others. But they always kick and scream and raise hell, so we have to clamp them. I think they should learn to take what they get.

Sometimes it's easy enough just to shove a shirt in their mouths. We have to be careful not to use our hands or else they might bite us. We don't have a lot of the high-tech gear. We haven't been given night-vision glasses. We don't even have electric cattle prods. We've put in requests, but the supervisors always drag their heels.

Raoul's a little soft. We just shove a stick under his jaw and push his head so far back that he can't scream. I just don't like the screaming. His neck stretches so far that he looks a little like one of those birds that fly high across the sky. The religious medal is caught between his teeth. He sucks on it, bites on it with his teeth. It is a tiny gold disc. We push his neck back so far that the gold chain snaps.

He coughs and splutters and the little religious medal falls from his mouth, rolls off the tarmac, into the sand.

You can tell a lot by a person's eyes. Raoul's are huge and brown.

That little disc of cheap gold probably means a lot to him. There's spittle at the corner of his mouth. He thrashes so hard that the stick at his neck slips, and his head bobs free. He screams and we kick him, once in the head, once in the ankles, and once in the balls. We clamp his mouth and shove the stick even harder under his neck.

We carry him off the end of the tarmac. Let his gold medal rot back there in the sand, we don't care.

We have two at Raoul's head, two at his feet and two at his side, his silence to keep. I control the stick. There's a lot of precision in that. You have to get it right at the base of his neck so it lodges hard. His body goes limp for a second and he's much easier to carry.

He's probably trying to figure a way to escape. They always try to lull us into a false sense of security. I'm no fool. I put a knee in his ribcage to remind him. He recoils. That'll teach him.

We step into the circle of spray that comes from the Water Machine.

It's cool on our shoulders. It almost makes you feel at peace. We slam Raoul up against the water pipe and strap him there. Belts work best. Rope tends to rot and fray.

The water is enough to drive you mad when you sit underneath it. Raoul tries to wriggle free. We take turns hitting him with sticks. It could be worse. It was worse for me, that's for sure. When I was captured in the old days, they took me to the Spin Machine. On the Spin Machine they make you lie down and prop your head out over the edge. Each time you turn they hit your head until it's a bloody mess.

We have to be careful. There's been some problems. There are new guidelines. The supervisors brought them out. So now we hit Raoul just enough that there won't be any blood. Blood is the worst of all. I hate having to explain the blood to the supervisors.

The Spin Machine is in the west, the Ropes are in the north for body burns, and the Tunnels in the south for the rats. Depending on how we feel, we use them all. Sometimes we take them from one to the other. I hate when they cry. It's worse than screaming. They should take it.

Me, I took it. Raoul should learn from me. But he's never going to listen. That's the problem with people like Raoul. They never learn to listen. They need to have a stick shoved under their neck and their bodies strapped to the water machine and then they need to be beaten.

That's the only way they learn. Then they don't cry anymore. And when they've had enough they come on our side.

I can see it in Raoul's eyes. The pupils are not so big anymore.

They're narrow and tight and glassy. He's beginning to understand. A few more kicks, a few more whacks, and then he'll know. A little trickle of snot slides down his chin where his medal was. That's the good thing about the water machine. The water wipes the snot and the marks away. Nobody knows.

Get up, Raoul.

He whimpers and falls.

Please, he says again, please.

He goes scurrying up the tarmac towards the sand. He falls down, looking for his medal and chain. We laugh. He's looking in the wrong place. That's hilarious. That's the funniest thing that's happened all day.

It's almost supervisor time. I hate supervisor time as much as screaming. They want to keep the rules complicated. They're always trying to muddy the waters. Then they come along and unlock the gates and shout, Come on, guys, come on, hurry up kids, time for dinner! Oh look George you got mud on your hat! Oh look Richard you tore your trousers. Oh look Carl, you forgot your new toy. Oh look Raoul you must've dropped your gold chain! They're thick, the supervisors.

That's what they are. They're mean and thick and they always arrive late. And then they drag us home kicking.

One of these days we're going to turn on them. That's what we're going to do, me and Raoul, we're going to get them. We'll buy our own cattle prods, wait'll you see. We'll get our night-vision glasses. That's a fact, it's a known fact, and who's going to stop us?

'A BLACK AND WHITE PRIESTLY GARB TOPPED OFF BY A DERISORY HAG'S WIG'

by Eugene McCabe

Everyone has the right to
recognition everywhere
as a person before the law.

Mick O'Dea

In 1949 I spent a year studying for the bar at the King's Inns and passed that first-year examination. Freddie Morris was the only budding barrister I knew. We shared the same hostel, a student seminary of sorts. Partaking of daily communion was an unwritten obligation to suppress, I imagine, other seminal inclinations. The hostel was run by a half-cracked Benedictine monk nicknamed Mad Muffins. I and other lie-in-bed suspects were not daily communicants.

As part of that first-year course we had to attend a working session at the Four Courts. What happened that morning left me more than disenchanted with the majesty of the law. There were a series of forgettable cases. Then a small boned, arthritic woman in her late seventies was led in by a large guard. Her crime, read out at length in Garda-speak, was followed by a heavy silence from the bench, followed by a session of obscene badgering. The following is a recreated essence:

'Do you understand the gravity of your crime, madam?'

A nod.

'Have you no voice?'

The guard intervened to say that the defendant had not spoken since taken into custody.

'Very well, you will answer with a nod or head shake. Do you believe in the hereafter?'

A nod.

'You must know that suicide is a passport to hell?'

A mix of nod and head shake.

'You left a shameful note; it's here before me. Have you any idea of the suffering inflicted on your family and friends by your selfish attempt?'

A head shake.

'Have you confessed?'

A nod.

There followed another grave silence till tears flowed down the wrinkled face of the criminal. Then the summing up and judgment: 'In this case I will not apply the full rigor of the law but be mindful, madam, if you appear before me again on this charge you'll leave me no choice.'

Then loudly: 'Do you understand me?'

A final nod.

'Take her down, guard.'

As the poor woman was not docked but standing below this bullying brute it was hard to imagine where she was being taken down to; a cell under the Four Courts? Back to her dark companions, grief, shame, loneliness and despair? Someone behind me muttered 'Jesus!'

Like the most of us there, I imagined nothing could be more remote from the compassion of Christ. Of course, it's been humanely reformed and the word depression is now tacked on to the wisdom of their lordships, legal and episcopal.

Present also in that Benedictine hostel were two white South Africans. Marron and Caffrey, studying medicine at The Pots Hall on Stephen's Green. Marron, I remember, was a great admirer of Frances Parkinson Keyes and dismissed James Joyce as a writer of 'dull stuff'. On a bus heading out to the hostel, a black man (rare in Ireland in those days) got on somewhere along Palmerston Road and sat facing us at the back. The two South Africans stood immediately and pressed the stop bell, their expressions and body language full of revulsion. As I remained seated, Marron said in a low, drawling voice meant to be overheard: 'Are you colour-blind, McCabe?'

I found it hard to believe what I'd heard. As the bus drew away I apologised directly for the gross insult. The black man did

not respond, deliberately looking past me. It was as though I
hadn't spoken. Understandably. I was sitting alongside and
obviously knew the white trash that had demeaned him publicly.
This was when judicial murder was at its peak in South Africa.
Regardless of origin (Africa, America, Australia, India, China)
that man had as much right 'before the law' at that time as we
native Irish had for centuries under the English crown. None.
Both Marron and Caffrey were first-generation Irish.

There is a notion abroad about the muscular independence
of the judiciary. Trotted out like holy writ, the law has been
shackled throughout history to the powers that be. Thomas More
and his Tudor monarch are an obvious example. You obey a
tyrannical executive or die, or, if lucky, go into exile. In our own
time, Charlie Haughey could and did intimidate banks, senior
revenue officials, big business and cowering backbenchers. Bertie
knew every slither of his shirty boss and kept his counsel. The
obverse of 'everyone's right as a person before the law' is: no one
has a right to bring the law to a standstill by denial, delay or
mendacious obfuscation. The Punch and Judy tribunal continues
to bore the public and squeeze millions from the national purse.
In truth, Judge Judy would see through the nonsense and dismiss
it with a few sharp questions and an even sharper judgment.

I've just read Cormac McCarthy's unnerving morality tale,
No Country for Old Men. Somewhere near the end, Sheriff Bell
ruminates: 'A lawyer once told me in law school they try to teach
you not to worry about right and wrong but just follow the law
and I said I wasn't so sure about that.'

Nor I suspect are most of us. No one doubts the everyday
integrity and necessary good work of the judiciary in most
democracies, but we all know or should be reminded how easily
such rights can evaporate. Check the internet for the

machinations of German law under Hitler's rule.

There's an endless choice of texts. One caught my eye:

> Hitler's justice: 'About blurring the line between lawful and unlawful conduct, the argument being that the Nazi Judiciary acted in a criminal manner.'

Old Denning with his foolish pronouncement about 'an appalling vista' must have been blind to recent history and the 'criminal manner' emanating from the Eagle's Nest, Stalin's Kremlin, Il Duce Palace and Chairman Mao's wee red bible. All judiciaries are corruptible and will bend for the German jackboot, Mr Bush's 'big stick' and rendition, Mr Heath dispatching the wretched Widgery to exonerate daylight murder, or Mrs Thatcher thumbing her nose at dying hunger strikers before clasping the beloved murderer Pinochet to her warrior breast. It has always been thus; always will be thus. The ordinary citizen is in thrall, in our case, to creatures with archaic blather aping their colleagues across the water, dressed up in black and white priestly garb topped off by a derisory hag's wig. The point of this fancy dress is to overawe some flawed Paddy or Patricia about the efficacy of his or her rights in the presence of such august personages.

Shakespeare's view of mankind and about judges and the law in general are balanced:

> I cannot tell what you and other men
> Think of this life; but, for my single self,
> I had as lief not be as live to be
> In awe of such a thing as I myself.

Alerting lines that cover his jaundiced opinion, not only of the law, but can be referenced to political, legal, religious or nowadays medical power anywhere at any time. The use of ideology, the Bible or Koran to degrade human rights (they use a tip-up lorry of stones nowadays in Saudi to punish 'the woman taken in adultery') to dominate, exterminate, burn or lash those who disagree about fixed cultural or religious notions is not about to change. Legal barbarity is still universal in vast areas of the world, and although human rights should be available to all man and womankind, this ideal is unlikely or near likely to be achieved. Is this a negative? One hundred and one percent. I do not believe 'the poor forked animal' can or will change much before or after the coming apocalypse.

Sometime in the seventies, during the height of the civil rights marches in America, we watched a programme that included The Supremes singing 'There's a Place For Us'. To this moment I can recall the enormous emotional impact of that song and those three beautiful black girls singing with unparalleled intensity. I can remember thinking at the time there will be a place for them and some day perhaps a United Africa will have its place in the world. Then a small dissenting voice at the time, and more so since, whispered: Moryah!

Everyone has the right to recognition everywhere as a person before the law.

LOW RESOLUTION

by Claire Kilroy

ARTICLE 7

All are equal before the
law and are entitled without
any discrimination to equal
protection of the law.
All are entitled to equal
protection against any
discrimination in violation
of this declaration and
against any incitement
to such discrimination.

'This train is for,' said the DART voice.

'Bray,' said the lads.

'Bray,' said the DART voice for the thicks.

The lads laughed. Bray was funny. Everything was funny after four tins. 'We're in the second last carriage,' Max was saying into his phone. He pulled a face. 'How would I know how many carriages the train has? I'm not the fucking oracle.' Max snapped the phone shut.

The lads fell quiet to keep an eye out for Aran when the platform at Sutton rolled into sight. They scanned the faces of waiting commuters who were shuffling blankly towards the train like zombies. 'There he is,' said Macdara, pointing down the far end where Aran was running in their direction, cutting easily through the crowd, his shirt collar turned up, his jeans belted low, straw-coloured hair sculpted into a fin. It was Saturday night.

The lads nearly broke their holes laughing when Aran sailed right past their window and boarded the carriage beyond. Even the girls in the seats opposite giggled. That was the first thing Aran saw when he opened the internal carriage door as the train rattled through back gardens in Bayside: the pretty girl in the white top smiling at him. Then the pretty girl looking shyly away.

It was about four drinks before he managed to get talking to her. The girl had smiled at him again when they found themselves in the queue for the same club on D'Olier Street, but she'd looked down at her feet before he got a chance to smile back. Aran had looked down at her feet too. Shoes way too big for her. Her friends were giggling again, elbowing her, whispering. Max kept prodding him in the arse. 'Get off me, Gaylord,' Aran warned him, but when he turned back, the girl was gone and the bouncer was demanding to see some ID.

He found the girl later standing on her own at the edge of the dance floor, gripping a bottle of WKD Blue. No sign of the giggling mates. 'Alright in here, isn't it?' Aran shouted at her.

'Yeah,' she shouted back, spilling smiles all over the place, 'it's deadly.'

He bought her a second WKD, then a third. Six lids a pop. He liked acting the big guy. The girl was younger than him, sixteen maybe, no money of her own yet, but Aran was flush from his part-time job, and wanted the world to know it.

They went out for a smoke in the corralled-off area of pavement on D'Olier Street, and Aran told the girl about his car. 'Deadly,' she kept saying. He offered to take her for a drive sometime, anywhere she wanted to go. The quarry, Dollymount, name it. A noisy fleet of Nitelinks pulled up to the kerb, and Aran got a notion into his head, a spur of the moment thing. 'Hey,' he said, 'let's jump on the 31.'

The girl looked nonplussed. 'What about my friends?' She was swaying in her too-big heels.

Aran grinned. 'What about them?' He touched her face and moved in for a kiss. That's how these things start. Easy.

'You're after missing your stop,' the girl said when Sutton Cross had come and gone.

'Don't worry about it,' Aran told her, and kissed her again. 'Don't you worry about a thing.' Their phones were yapping at each other like small dogs, but they paid them no attention. They got out at the harbour, though neither of them lived down there. Aran held the girl's hand in his left hand and her big sister's shoes in his right as the pair clambered across the boulders buttressing East Pier. It was a warm June night. The sky was navy, already brightening, Ireland's Eye a black sea monster drifting past.

Aran spread his jacket out on a large flat rock and the girl sat in the crook of his arm to share a joint. They laughed and talked and threw pebbles into the sea. When the girl shivered, Aran wrapped himself around her and she sort of eased against him. He cupped her head and laid her back, lowering his weight carefully down on her. Her head lolled drunkenly, but she was still smiling, still lovely. 'Aw yeah,' he said. 'Aw yeah,' he said. 'Aw yeah.'

'What have I reared?' his mother asked the ceiling when the two Guards had left. She bit hard on the knuckle of her index finger. Statutory rape. Jesus, Mary and Joseph.

I can hardly bear to look at you, his father wanted to tell his son, but didn't open his mouth. Instead, he phoned his solicitor and outlined the situation. 'The father is pressing charges,' he told him. Gerald said he'd come around to the house immediately.

'She didn't look thirteen,' Aran kept protesting.

'She will when she's sitting in front of that jury,' Gerald told the family grimly, taking out his legal pad.

The fact that the girl had lied her way into a nightclub for over-eighteens helped their defence enormously. The manager of the club testified that the false photo identification the girl had produced at the door was a professional job, not the handiwork of a schoolgirl. It was, however, the video footage of the two teenagers dancing recorded by Max on his mobile phone that convinced the jury that the whole unfortunate incident was an honest mistake on the defendant's part.

Aran's father was relieved to concede that, if anything, the girl looked more mature in the jerky, low resolution video than his gawky, plastered, moronic son, throwing himself around the dance floor with no heed to the beat of the music, the jeans hanging off his backside and that inane tuft of hair on his head. What have I reared? his mother wondered again. The girl may have been thirteen, but she didn't look thirteen, the jury concluded, and therefore she lost the rights due to a minor. Besides, it wasn't like she was a virgin.

The two families hung back in their respective barristers' chambers waiting for the other family to vacate the court buildings first. An hour apiece they gave it, to be safe. Gerald stepped outside, and reported that the coast was clear. He put his hand on Aran's shoulder as the lad left. A rape conviction would have destroyed his future, but Aran felt no relief.

Both parties rounded the corner into the entrance hall at the same time. They drew up sharply when they saw each other, then lowered their eyes and ploughed on, making their way down the steps together, she baby-faced without her make-up, and he awkward in a suit he wouldn't fill for a few years yet, the one as big a child as the other.

'CUSTER NEVER HAD TO GO IN FRONT OF A TRIBUNAL'

by Roddy Doyle

ARTICLE 8

Everyone has the right
to an effective remedy
by the competent national
tribunals for acts violating
the fundamental rights
granted him by the
constitution or by law.

He checked his pockets. He had his money, his keys. Although he didn't really need keys – he hadn't driven a car in years. But he liked the weight of them, and the key ring was a present from his son-in-law.

– So, what's on this morning? he asked.

– The Cabinet breakfast.

– Grand.

– The Lisbon referendum, the HSE –

– I'm going to get those letters tattooed across my arse.

– Tibet and the Dublin Port Tunnel.

– That's not too bad, he said. – We'll be out before Mary H is finished her porridge. What then?

– A launch.

– Oh, God.

– No, no, it's fine. Cherish the Child Week. Photo op. Twenty children.

– Oh, grand.

He loved kids. He absolutely loved kids. He loved getting in among them and chatting. And the photos, when they did the rabbit's ears behind his head and he pretended to be shocked and it made them laugh. And there was always one messer, one great messer. Some kid he'd remember for the rest of the day – something the kid would say, or the look in his eyes. Something like that, to keep him going.

A great way to start the day.

He regretted it sometimes. He wished he'd spent more time with his own –

– Stop, he said.

That was beginning to creep in – the talking out loud to himself. Just the odd word. Still though, it could be the wrong word. At the wrong time. To the wrong man. Or woman. He'd have to be more careful.

But he was already as careful as he could be. He even slept carefully.

He had a quick look in the mirror. Nothing too searching; he wasn't alone. It was one thing he hated – the sneering at his use of cosmetics. Bastards. As if flaking skin was a badge of honour.

He looked tired – he was tired. He smiled – it still worked.

– And then? he said.

– A new ambassador. Five minutes.

– Where from?

– Em –

– You have to check. It must be tiny.

– Austria.

– Grand, he said. – Don't mention the war.

He looked at his watch. He had a few minutes. Breakfast with the Cabinet, though – Jesus.

– So, he said. – Austria. What then?

– The Universal Declaration of Human Rights.

– I'm not writing it, am I? He was smiling.

– No, she said. – Just reading it. One of the Articles. There are – let me see.

– Thirty, he said. – I remember. It's the sixtieth anniversary. And I'm reading one of the Articles. Me and twenty-nine other vital people. I hope they gave me Number 1.

– No.

– No?

– Actually, you're Number 8.

He laughed.

– What bollix got Number 1? Let me guess – Bono.

– Heaney.

– Bono got Number 2.

– Three.

– Who got 2?

– Your daughter.

He laughed again. He held his head back, so he could really let go of it.

The day was getting better and better.

– And her poor oul' da, he said. – He's only Number 8.

– 'Fraid so.

– Read it out there for us. I'll have to give it the oul' MacLiammóir.

– It's only two lines.

– I can cope with that.

She read.

– Everyone has the right to an effective remedy by the competent national tribunals for acts violating the fundamental rights granted him by the constitution or by law.

She stopped.

– That's it, she said. – Are you all right?

His mouth eventually opened. A word came out.

– Tri –

He tried again.

– Tribunals?

She looked back down at the page.

– Yes.

– I can't read that.

– I'm sure you could swap with your daughter –

– No, no, he said. – No. I can't do that either. I can't object. It's the Universal Declaration of Human Rights. I can't not do it. Bollix to it, anyway. Give it to me again there.

She read it again.

– I'm asking for tribunals, he said. – That's what I'll be saying, isn't it? Basically. Isn't it?

– Yes, she said. – But not literally. Not in the Irish sense.

– Tribunals, though.

– Courts of appeal. A transparent judicial system.

– I know!

He held up his hands.

– Sorry, he said. – I'm very sorry.

– I understand.

– No, he said. – I was rude. I'm sorry.

He put his hands to his head.

– But tribunals!

His scalp felt a bit dry.

– They'll be waiting.

– They?

– The lads with the click-clicks. And the gentlemen and lezzers of the press. Waiting.

– I suppose they will.

– It's an ambush, he said. – A feckin' ambush. Custer didn't know the half of it.

– I suppose not.

– Custer never had to go in front of a tribunal. Did he?

– I'm not really all that familiar with the history of the Wild West, she said.

He looked at her.

– I did home economics, she told him.

He smiled.

– Fair enough, he said. – Fair enough. But I bet Custer never had to explain how he paid for his curtains or his patio furniture.

He stopped smiling.

– Who put me down to read 8, though?

– I'm not sure.

— Some bollix in Justice, he said. — What number did Lenihan get? She looked at the page.

— 29.

— That's something, anyway, he said. — He's nearly on the sub's bench. What about O'Dea?

— He doesn't seem to be on the list.

— Grand, he said. — And Biffo?

— Number 9.

— Close, he said. — There's no mention of tribunals in his one, I'd say, is there?

— No.

— Or tax-evading publican brothers, no?

— No.

— No, of course not.

He sighed. He tried to smile.

— Imagine that, he said. — I'm being stabbed in the back by Amnesty International.

He had another quick gawk in the mirror. He looked no different. Less tired maybe, the eyes a bit wild. But they suited him.

— Who got Number 7?

— Joe Duffy.

— Oh, good night. Good afternoon to you. Number 30?

She looked at the page.

— Gerry Hutch.

— Jesus Christ, what band is he in?

— He's —

— I know, I know. The star of *Prime Time* and the *Sunday World*.

His shoulders were at him. He took off his jacket. He looked at the watch. He still had a minute. He took out his Man Utd key ring. He hopped it up and down on his palm. He put it back in his trouser pocket.

– The words that'll haunt me for the rest of my life, he said. – Tribunal. Sterling.

– Arsenal.

– Now you're talking. Bastards.

He put the jacket back on.

– I'd ban the tribunals, he said. – I would. Human rights, me arse. Big pay days for middle class, Jesuit-educated Fine Gaelers and –

He whispered the letters.

– PDs.

He sighed again.

– I did nothing wrong.

– I know, she said.

– A house for two poor oul' dears.

– I know.

– Seriously, he said. – I hadn't a clue what I was doing those years. After – you know, the breakup. It takes years to get over something like that.

One last look in the mirror. He was all right. He didn't look the way he felt – he wasn't sure how he felt. He wanted to laugh – part of him did. But most of him didn't. And a part of him wanted to cry.

– And now I've to go out there with Bono and the sandal brigade and call for even more tribunals.

He looked at his watch.

– Let's go, he said. – We can't be late for the Cabinet.

She opened the door.
He stopped.
– Are you alright? she asked.
– Fuck this, he said. – Call a press conference.
He took off his jacket. He lobbed it across the room.
– I'm resigning.

ONE DAY IN THE LIFE OF . . .

by Tom Humphries

ARTICLE 9

No one shall be subjected
to arbitrary arrest,
detention or exile.

The phone is switched to silent out of respect for my Mexican pedicurist. Now though, the little screen keeps flashing on and off incessantly. Seán Love from Amnesty calling. Jesus. Not today. Read me my rights somebody.

I subvert a lot of governments so I find it wise to keep onside with Amnesty International. Just in case. I mean who ya gonna call? Micheál Martin?

To be honest, though, they are hard work, the Amnesty crowd. Like drinking with an op-ed page. I look at Love's name flashing menacingly. I try to focus. He ain't calling with a mother-in-law joke. That's for sure.

Just how are things going with the plight of the repressed Azerbaijani Socialist Brotherhood of Carpet Weavers? Is that Love's real name or a porn star name which he made up for himself? Maybe they want me to rescue somebody. Cool! Shit. I'm so hungry. Time for the glycolic wrap. Rosita? Heel balm? Fan-tast-ico! Focus.

Morning at Ronaldo's. As usual, at 9.30 AM reveille was sounded by the jingle jangle of a hammer striking an antique triangle hanging up near the staff quarters of a large reconverted building along the banks of the Manchester ship canal.

Jeeves (for it was she) pushed back the curtains flooding the room with light before he was ready. In a cruel, unusual and unnecessarily chirpy tone she interrogated Ronaldo as to whether or not he would enjoy it if she microwaved a couple of those In-An-Instant Croissants.

'I would love that,' said Ronaldo. 'Love it.'

He reached for his bedside book, Kevin Keegan, Reluctant Messiah *and smiled. A thousand watts of teeth.*

*In fifteen minutes he would leave his bed to face the world.
This would be the worst day of his life. Again. For now,
though, the day would start like every other. Chow time.*

Love has an idea. (Memo to self: write U2 a song with working
title 'Love Has an Idea'.)

'As you know,' he says, '2008 is the sixtieth anniversary of the
Universal Declaration of Human Rights.'

'Yup, yup, Love,' I say, '*naturellement.*'

Anyway Love has stumbled on this Declaration of Human
Rights thing and with a metaphorical but camp flourish he fans
the entire deck of articles in front of me and tells me to pick an
article, any article.

'And?'

'Then you can write about it! Ta da!'

He's trying to make himself sound like Derek Mooney on the
Lotto programme. Which is sad. I know Derek and you, Love,
are no Mooney.

'Pick a number between one and thirty,' he says. No mention
of a fee. No mention of free flights to anyplace warm where
people might be incarcerated. Typical Amnesty stunt. Think not
for the first time of applying for a transfer to some other
bleeding-heart group. I know that Love will never let me go.
(Memo to self: scrap 'Love Has an Idea'. This is better.)

I pick a number.

'Tough,' says Love. (Bono, just scribble these down as I come up
with them, pet. Tough says love. Tough love shoo doo be dooby.)

'That one is gone.'

I pick another number.

'Not your day,' says Love. (That one's for you, Donna and
Joseph. Respect.)

Finally, because his credit is running out, he gets desperate.

'Look. Love Potion Number?'

'You're endorsing a politically correct scent, Love? Eau de Seán Luuurve?'

'No. The song, you fat twat.'

Sometimes Love is not as politically correct as he makes himself out to be. Not when it comes to the forgotten victims of fluid retention.

'Nine?' I say, muttering the word 'baldy' under my breath.

'All yours,' he says. 'Now Seamus Heaney is leading off Saturday, March 15th, doing an, ahem, an introductory essay,' he says, purring.

'Oh.'

He knows that this hurts.

Heaney is alright. But I think everyone sucks up to him out of sympathy because he is old and he never got larged up on Richard and Judy. This is more of the same. He gets to lead the peloton out.

Anyway, I thought this was going to be a sportswriter's thing. Love lists off the writers involved. Mainly no-marks who cater for the cobwebbed reading room/no friends set. All of them panting for their big break, getting some of their drear into the paper. On a Saturday too. Saturday is the day we have the 'What's Hot and What's Not' guide. Who needs this?

The only other sporting connection is Neil Jordan, and it's so long since he played for the Bulls he is mostly forgotten about. Hot? Not!

There was a bruised, lowering sky over the training ground when Ronaldo arrived. His right nipple worryingly reddened from the chafing of the seat belt across his chest. He examined himself tenderly. He had often been accused of feigning injury. If people only knew the truth. In here you got yourself well, kept your injuries to yourself, the physio and the masseuse, just people you could trust.

He'd had to ask Jeeves (who would work for Portuguese players but not those Spaniards who pronounced her name Heeves, no way Joe-Say) to pour hot water on the Ferrari 275 GTB/4 Berlinetta to take away the white cobwebs of hoar frost which scabbed the windscreen. And then he'd brought the Lamborghini Miura anyway. Rooney had a Ferrari. It hurt to see Mr Potato Head pull in beside him with the same wheels.

Later, out in the field, which was needlessly bobbly, he had to wear his gloves as a meagre shield against the cold which swept in from the Steppes or the Pennines or someplace he had been told about but he could no longer remember. Alps?

They had just begun work when O'Shea, an old lag, harmless, sidled up to him out of view of the boss man.

'I don't like it here,' hissed O'Shea, staring straight down the field. 'I'm tired of being afraid all the time. I've decided not to stay. I doubt they'll kick up any fuss. Not for an old centre half like me.'

Ronaldo moved away swiftly. Transfer deadline day, O'Shea thought he was busting out. It couldn't happen. Not today. No way, J. O'Shea. The Madrid connection had taken patient months to set up. His agent had compromised his dignity with the Spaniards and would have to live with that.

They were barking now like bulldogs. Drill time. Not today. Not today, thought Ronaldo, and suddenly he was airborne, his body convulsing and contorted in the air, his face grimacing with agony before he fell to earth again *clutching his right ankle. He lay there writhing.*

As they stretchered him off toward the infirmary he stared at the sky, inviting now, somehow. He spoke softly and only those bearing his weight could hear him.

'I have to remind myself,' he said, 'that some birds aren't meant to be caged. Their feathers are just too bright. And when they fly away, (maybe, for example, to Real Madrid) the part of you that knows it was a sin to lock them up DOES rejoice. Still, the place you live in is that much more drab and empty than mine. Ha ha.'

The staff, screws, call them what you will, carrying the stretcher, exchanged glances. One rolled his eyes toward the same sky which was calling Ronaldo.

Not to carp on about Heaney but I once won the Writer of the Year gong at the Listowel Writers' Week. The big cahunas (I'm talking Myers here, O'Toole, some actual feminists) they were all in for it. And lost.

They tried to cover it up of course. Stalinist bastards. A sportswriter winning the Palme D'Or for an article about footie? They ran a paragraph in the paper of course. 'Sportswriter wins literary award'. It was below a story headlined 'Monkey types line from Hamlet'. They had the pic of the monkey placed in between the two stories so you couldn't really tell which story the picture belonged to.

I didn't care. Edna O'Brien (bless) handed over the prize and we both looked fabulous. She said breathily to me I reminded her of 'the Russian'. I didn't understand but pretty quick afterwards ole Edna and me had each other roaring. It was like a tigress getting it on with a polar bear, other people in the bar said afterwards. Aha.

I know Heaney won that IKEA prize thing but that's the gloomy Scandinavians for you. Even in that league he's no Mankell. I know Henning Mankell and you Heaney are no Henning.

Plus there's bad blood between Heaney and myself since last year's pro-am Ultimate Frisbee tournament at the Community Games in Mosney. Any man who cheats at Ultimate hasn't got a poetic soul. But he is that ruthless.

Seamus Big Booty Heaney?

Yeah right.

Love knows all this of course. He's trying to get inside my head. So for months I do nothing.

He hears them before he sees them. The sound of many boots in the corridor. Coming for him this time. He lies there, perfectly still, pretending to be dead. His brain oozes regret. He remembered the words of O'Shea. They came for Stam, I said nothing. The Irishman was right. Say nothing.

The door bursts open. Boss. He strides, ruddy but magnificent, to the end of the bed. All other lags behind him. 'I know you're not deed, sonnae,' he says. Gang patois.

Ronaldo rubs his eyes and sits up suddenly as though from a dream. They form a large semi-circle around his bed. They are smiling thinly. So this is how it happens. This is endgame.

'Here,' says Boss. And he drops a brown envelope on Ronaldo's chest. No tenderness.

He wishes he were at home in the envelope-opening room. The thoughts of it make his eyes well. He busies himself with the envelope. A document falls out. In big writing on the cover page are the words Fat New Contract. With a jingle jangle the bling falls out too. A perfect gold necklace with ring and bracelet to match. The lags begin a rhythmic clapping.

Some kind of native spiritual thing, thinks Ronaldo. He holds the gold chain to his neck and tears run down his tanned cheeks.

Boss: 'You gonnae get used to wearin' them chains after awhile, son. Don't you never stop listenin' to them clinking, cause they gonnae remind you of what I've been saying – for your own good.'

Ronaldo: 'I wish you'd stop being so good to me, boss. Someday I'll fly away.'

Boss (blushing and cuffing him gently): 'Aw don't you ever talk that way to me. Never! Never!'

Boss turns now and he addresses the team, the chain gang, call these men what you will.

'What we've got here men is a failure to communicate. Some men, you just can't reach without going through their agents. So you get what we had here last week – which is the way he wants it. Well, he gets it!'

And now they step forward and in their rough, inarticulate way they each tousle Ronaldo's hair before turning to go.

Soon it will just be Ronaldo and the Boss. He wishes they would just shake hands instead of messing with the hair. What the hell.

Months pass. One call from Love.

– Perhaps you could write about China.

– I want to write about camogie.

– Whatever.

Article 9.

No one shall be subjected to arbitrary arrest, detention or exile.

More months. Send Bono lyrics to original new work entitled 'I

Would Do Anything for Love, But I Won't Do That'.

Days later. Receive terse, pointed and frankly threatening e-mail from somebody called Hugh Linehan, Features Editor, the *Irish Times*.

'Tomorrow would be great. Not to labour the point, but we had a bunch of the writers down at Electric Picnic talking about how hard it was, and the one thing they all agreed on is they'd all wanted to do torture. I quote: "which f***er got torture?"'

Would like to edit Linehan's features. Spend wounded hour brooding on why they were all at Electric Picnic. Was Heaney doing his human beatbox thing? Soooo last year. Still, love watching Roddy Doyle rap. The guy is street. He is ghetto.

Torture! Ya!

Spend many hours writing hilarious waterboarding jokes. I mean real sidesplitters. A few thumbscrew gags. And (rim shot please!) finish the thing off with some crafty electrodes to the testicles patter, the lighter side of the deal. You know, dimmer switches and all. I write it so it rhymes too. Just to make Heaney look like the hack he is.

Smoke large cheroot. Flick back through e-mails before tackling Linehan.

E-mail from Love in the spam folder with all that penis enlargement stuff (price is going to fall isn't it?). Haven't got torture after all. Bastards. Who got torture? I have arbitrary arrest, detention and exile. They are bad apparently. Article 9 says so. So does Sepp Blatter.

No inspiration. I would do anything for Love. But I can't do this.

When he lay down that night Ronaldo went to sleep fully content. He'd had many strokes of luck that day. He had survived until tomorrow. His hair was responding to treatment. Rooney did his hammer.

A day without a dark cloud. Almost a happy day.

There were 3,653 days like that in the sentence of Cristiano Ronaldo dos Santos Aveiro. From the first blast of the hairdryer to the last blast of the hairdryer.

The three extra days were for leap years. His agent negotiated special leap year bonus packages, so that was ok.

Happy now Love? Bono pick up. Donna? Joseph?

THE ROUND HALL

by John Boyne

ARTICLE 10

Everyone is entitled in full
equality to a fair and public
hearing by an independent and
impartial tribunal, in the
determination of his rights
and obligations and of any
criminal charge against him.

It's early when he arrives at the courthouse and the doors are still locked. There's no press outside. That's a relief. He doesn't want to be one of those fat bastards, covering his eyes with a copy of that morning's *Irish Times*, being chased along the quays by photographers. He's nothing like them. He isn't fat, for one thing. He's so skinny that the ma says she's jealous of him. I don't know where you put it all, she tells him. The crisps and the cokes and the Galaxy bars. I only have to pass a sweet shop, she says.

Thank Christ the doors open and in he goes.

He sits and he waits.

'You're Francis Kelly, are you?'

He looks up to see a man of about sixty wearing a black cloak with a starched white collar, his arms full of files.

'Yes sir,' he says. 'Only I don't know why I'm –'

'I'm Mr Jones. I've been instructed on all the particulars. It's fairly cut and dry. You're pleading guilty?'

'I'm bleedin' innocent,' shouts Francis, jumping up so quickly that the barrister takes a step back in surprise.

'Yes but you're pleading guilty,' he says, stressing the 'p'. He speaks like someone who could name the fly-half for the Irish rugby team.

'No,' says Francis, shaking his head. 'I don't even know what this is about. I only got the letter on Friday and it told me to –'

'Stay here,' says the barrister, walking away. 'I'll be back shortly.'

Francis sits down again. It's cold in the Round Hall but a drop of sweat is working its way slowly down his arm. There was only one good shirt in the wardrobe this morning, the one he used to wear for school, so he'd put it on with the tie that the da left him in his will. If the ma had woken up and seen him leaving in it she would have looked at him. She'd probably have thought he was up in court.

He holds his left hand out in front of him and then his right and stares at them both. Am I going mad, he wonders, or is this one bigger than that one?

'What are you up for?'

There's a girl sitting next to him now. The state of her. An Adidas top and a big belly on her that she keeps one hand on. He looks at it and looks at her and feels his face blush.

Pregnant girls always make him nervous. He's never done it himself. Not with someone else anyway.

'Nothing,' he says.

'You're not here for nothing,' she says. 'Or you wouldn't be here at all.'

'I'm waiting on someone,' he says, thinking this isn't a lie anyway, since he's waiting for the barrister to come back.

'Have you got a light?'

'There's no smoking in here, Mary,' says a stern voice from the girl's left and he looks up and sees a big garda there, a woman garda, her right hand linked to the girl's left by a handcuff. 'And don't you know that smoking's no good for that baby of yours?'

'Banging me up for the next fifteen years won't do her much good either, will it?' asks the girl, looking like she wants to put the cigarette out in the garda's eye.

'What are you up for?' asks Francis.

'I beat up my boyfriend,' she says with a shrug. 'I hit him with a poker. They're saying it was attempted murder.'

'Jesus,' says Francis.

'I didn't do it,' she says calmly, as if they're in a play and that's her next line.

He shakes his head and takes his mobile out, looks at it, but doesn't turn it on. He knows there'll be a message from Ms Geraghty asking him where he is, why he isn't in by now, will he phone if there's a problem. And there'll be another from the ma saying that Ms Geraghty's been on the blower looking for him. He doesn't want to talk to either of them.

'Francis.' The barrister's back now with even more files. 'Come with me, will you?' He jumps up and follows him through a door. It's like a church in here, he thinks, looking around. All the pews in a row and an altar up ahead. People praying for forgiveness. He tries to listen as the barrister talks to the judge but there's an awful lot of big words being used and none of them make sense. 'Sit down there,' says a garda, pushing him into a seat at the front. He thinks back to when he was an altar boy. He never knew when to stand, when to sit, when to kneel. It used to drive the priest mad. 'You're an awful creature,' he'd tell him in the sacristy afterwards, going mad even though no one ever explained what he'd done wrong and why he was in trouble.

'The best we can hope for is a suspended sentence,' says Mr Jones, coming over and putting a hand on his shoulder. 'We can go for mitigating circumstances. You'll be on a good behaviour bond though and if you try to leave –'

'What?' cries Francis, his eyes opening wide. 'I don't even know –'

'Silence over there,' roars the judge, who's a hundred years old if he's a day.

'Apologies, your honour,' says the barrister in reply, standing up, then leaning down again. He's up and down like a jack-in-the-box, this lad. 'Are you going to be this difficult all the way through?' he asks.

'I'm not being difficult,' says Francis. 'But I got the letter, right, and I came here like I was told, only no one's told me –'

'Ah here,' says the barrister, breathing a great breeze of cheese and onion crisps in Francis's face before turning around and marching back up to the front.

Francis hasn't allowed himself to think about this until now but he can't help it. Jail. Jesus, even the idea of it. God knows what they'd do to him in there. He saw a documentary about Mountjoy once on the telly, back when the da was alive, and there were four of them in a cell no bigger than his bedroom, looking at the camera as if it had just insulted their mothers. They wore ratty gray jumpers and looked like they only shaved once every few weeks. 'You know what they get up to in there, don't you?' the da had asked him. 'Any port in a storm.'

And then there was that book, the one he read for the Junior Cert a few years back. Your man, Pip, running through the graveyard and the convict grabbing him and asking for his wittles. He isn't like that. He hasn't done anything. He needs someone to listen to him.

'Right, we're done,' says the barrister, coming back now with a garda standing next to him. 'We couldn't get the suspended sentence in the end, I'm afraid. That's me three–nil down on the week.'

'Put out your hands, lad,' says the garda, taking a pair of handcuffs from his belt and locking them around Francis's wrists.

'But no one's even asked me anything yet,' says Francis as he's pulled out of his seat and through the door. 'There's supposed to be a trial at least.' They're out in the Round Hall again now. The pregnant girl's walking through the door into Court no. 3. She's got some arse on her, he'll give her that.

'A trial?' asks the barrister, laughing. 'You've been watching too much TV, son.'

Francis stares at him, his mouth hanging open, until he feels himself being yanked to his right and he has to pick up his feet as he's dragged through another set of doors and out onto a side street. A van is waiting there with the back doors closed.

'This isn't right,' he cries but that just makes the garda walk even quicker and the handcuffs cut into his wrists. The doors open and it's dark inside. He can make out a few men huddled together, staring out at him, their eyes like cats'. They want their wittles. A minute later and he's inside with them, trying to jump up before the doors close again. 'You can't,' he shouts. 'You have to listen to me.'

And there's one now. A photographer. Standing a few feet away looking in at him as the doors close. He picks up his camera and puts it to his eye but hesitates, thinks better of it, and turns away.

'Help,' cries Francis as the doors slam and the van's ignition turns on.

'Help,' he says more quietly, turning to the men now who stare at him as if they're deciding what the fairest way is to carve him up.

'Help.'

The van pulls out onto the quays. It's gone ten o'clock by now. The traffic is only shocking.

ON 'THE ANATOMISATION OF AN UNKNOWN MAN' (1637) BY FRANS MIER

by John Connolly

ARTICLE 11

1. Everyone charged with a penal offence has the right to be presumed innocent until proved guilty according to the law in a public trial at which they have had all the guarantees necessary for their defence.

2. No one shall be held guilty of any penal offence on account of any act or omission which did not constitute a penal offence, under national or international law, at a time when it was committed. Nor shall a heavier penalty be imposed than the one that was applicable at the time the penal offence was committed.

Jim Fitzpatrick

I

The painting titled 'The Anatomisation of an Unknown Man' is one of the more obscure works by the minor Dutch painter, Frans Mier. It is an unusual piece, although its subject matter may be said to be typical of our time: the opening up of a body by what is, one initially assumes, a surgeon or anatomist, the light from a suspended lamp falling over the naked body of the anonymous man, his scalp peeled back to reveal his skull, his innards exposed as the anatomist's blade hangs suspended above him, ready to explore further the intricacies of his workings, the central physical component of the universe's rich complexity.

I was not long ago in England, and witnessed there the hanging of one Elizabeth Evans – Canberry Bess, they called her – a notorious murderer and cutpurse, who was taken with her partner, one Thomas Shearwood. Counterey Tom was hanged and then gibbeted at Gray's Inn fields, but it was the fate of Elizabeth Evans to be dissected after her death at the Barber-Surgeons' Hall, for the body of a woman is of more interest to the surgeons than the body of a man, and harder to come by. She wept and screamed as she was brought to the gallows, and cried out for a Christian burial, for the terror of the Hall was greater to her than that of the noose itself. Eventually, the hangman silenced her with a rag, for she was disturbing the crowd.

Something of her fear had communicated itself to the onlookers, though, for there was a commotion at the gallows, as I recall. Although the surgeons wore the guise of commoners, the crowd knew them for what they were, and a shout arose that the woman had suffered enough under the Law, and that she should have no further barbarities visited upon her, although I fear their concern was less for the dignity of her repose than the knowledge that the mob was to be deprived of the display of her carcass in chains at St Pancras, and the slow exposure of her bones at King's Cross. Still, the surgeons had their way for when the hangman was done with her, she was cut down and stripped of her apparel, then laid naked in a chest and thrown into a cart. From there, she was carried to the Hall near unto Cripplegate. For a penny, I was permitted, with others, to watch as the surgeons went about their work, and a revelation it was to me.

But I digress. I merely speak of it to stress that Mier's painting cannot be understood in isolation. It is a record of our time, and should be seen in the context of the work of Valverde and Estienne, of Spigelius and Berrettini and Berengarius, those other great illustrators of the inner mysteries of our corporeal form.

Yet look closer and it becomes clear that the subject of Mier's painting is not as it first appears. The unknown man's face is contorted in its final agony, but there is no visible sign of strangulation, and his neck is unmarked. If he is a malefactor taken from the gallows, then by what means was his life ended? Although the light is dim, it is clear that his hands have been tied to the anatomist's table by means of stout rope. Only the right hand is visible, admittedly, but one would hardly secure one and not the other. On his wrist are gashes where he has struggled against his bonds, and blood pours from the table to the floor in great quantities. The dead do not bleed in this way.

And if this is truly a surgeon, then why does he not wear the attire of a learned man? Why does he labour alone in some dank place, and not in a hall or theatre? Where are his peers? Why are there no other men of science, no assistants, no curious onlookers enjoying their penny's worth? This, it would appear, is secret work.

Look: there, in the corner, behind the anatomist, head tilted to stare down at the dissected man. Is that not the head and upper body of a woman? Her left hand is raised to her mouth, and her eyes are wide with grief and horror, but here too a rope is visible. She is also restrained, although not so firmly as the anatomist's victim. Yes, perhaps 'victim' is the word, for the only conclusion to be drawn is that the man on the table has suffered under the knife. This is no corpse from the gallows, and this is not a dissection.

This is something much worse.

II

The question of attribution is always difficult in such circumstances. It resembles, one supposes, the investigation into the commission of a crime. There are clues left behind by the murderer, and it is the work of an astute and careful observer to connect such evidence to the man responsible. The use of a single source of light, shining from right to left, is typical of Mier. So, too, is the elongation of the faces, so that they resemble wraiths more than people, as though their journey into the next life has already begun. The hands, by contrast, are clumsily rendered, those of the anatomist excepted. It may be that they are the efforts of others, for Mier would not be alone among artists in allowing his students to complete his paintings. But then it could also be that it is Mier's intention to draw our gaze to the anatomist's hands. There is a grace, a subtlety to the scientist's calling, and Mier is perhaps suggesting that these are skilled fingers holding the blade.

To Mier, this is an artist at work.

III

I admit that I have never seen the painting in question. I have only a vision of it in my mind based upon my knowledge of such matters. But why should that concern us? Is not imagining the first step towards bringing something into being? One must envisage it, and then one can begin to make it a reality. All great art commences with a vision, and perhaps it may be that the vision is closer to God than that which is ultimately created by the artist's brush. There will always be human flaws in the execution. Only in the mind can the artist achieve true perfection.

IV

It is possible that the painting called 'The Anatomisation of an Unknown Man' may not exist.

V

What is the identity of the woman? Why would someone force her to watch as a man is torn apart, compel her to listen to his screams as the blade takes him slowly, exquisitely apart? Surgeons and scientists do not torture in this way.

Thus, if we are not gazing upon a surgeon at work, then, for want of another word, we are looking at a murderer. He is older than the others in the picture, although not so old that his beard has turned grey. The woman, meanwhile, is beautiful; let there be no doubt of that. Mier was not a sentimental man, and would not have portrayed her as other than she was. The victim, too, is closer in age to the woman than the man. We can see it in his face, and in the once youthful perfection of his now ruined body.

Yes, perhaps he has the look of a Spaniard about him.

VI

I admit that Frans Mier may not exist.

VII

With this knowledge, gleaned from close examination of the work in question, let us now construct a narrative. The man with the knife is not a surgeon, although he might wish to be, but he has a curiosity about the nature of the human body that has led him to observe closely the attentions of the anatomists. The woman? Let us say: his wife, lovely yet unfaithful, fickle in her affections, weary of the ageing body that shares her bed and hungry for firmer flesh.

And the man on the table, then, is, or was, her lover. What if we were to suppose that the husband has discovered his wife's infidelity. Perhaps the young man is his apprentice, one whom he has trusted and loved as a substitute for the child that has never graced his marriage. Realising the nature of his betrayal, the master lures his apprentice to the cellar, where the table is waiting. No, wait: he drugs him with tainted wine, for the apprentice is younger and stronger than he is, and the master is unsure of his ability to overpower him. When the apprentice regains consciousness, woken by the screams of the woman trapped with him, he is powerless to move. He adds his voice to hers, but the walls are thick, and the cellar deep. There is no one to hear.

A figure advances, and the lamp catches the sharp blade, and the grim work begins.

VIII

So: this is our version of the truth, our answer to the question of attribution. I, Nicolaes Deyman, did kill my apprentice Mantegna. I anatomised him in my cellar, slowly taking him apart as though, like the physicians of old, I might be able to find some as yet unsuspected fifth humour within him, some black and malignant thing responsible for his betrayal. I did force my wife, my beloved Judith, to watch as I removed skin from flesh, and flesh from bone. When her lover was dead, I strangled her with a rope, and I wept as I did so.

I accept the justice and wisdom of the court's verdict: that my name should be struck from all titles and records and never uttered again; that I should be taken from this place and hanged in secret and then, while still breathing, that I should be handed over to the anatomists and carried to their great temple of learning, there to be taken apart while my heart beats so that the slow manner of my dying might contribute to the greater sum of human knowledge, and thereby make some recompense for my crimes. I ask only this: that an artist, a man of some small talent, might be permitted to observe and record all that transpires so the painting called 'The Anatomisation of an Unknown Man' might at last come into existence. After all, I have begun the work for him. I have imagined it. I have described it. I have given him his subject, and willed it into being.

For I, too, am an artist, in my way.

WHAT HARM?

by Lia Mills

So, I'm at her door. I found the number easy enough from the letterbox in the lobby, took the stairs to the fifth floor. I wanted time to think. What to do if I see her. What to say. I still don't know.

She throws open the door. 'You're late,' she says.

What? How did she know I'm here? She must've heard my heart, drumming on my ribs. Any minute now it'll jump out through my mouth and eat her.

'They usually send someone – older,' she says, eyeing how I'm dressed – trench coat, jeans and the Nikes I wear for school. I couldn't find my Uggs this morning.

I've seen her before, but not in real life. She's everyone's favourite model-turned-PR-babe, all over the news lately because of this stratospheric gig she put on for charity. Meta4 donated their hotel for a whole weekend. Their celebrity mates performed and hung out with the crowd, live on TV. Everyone in the country was trampling their grannies to get tickets. You couldn't get away from her picture or her voice promoting that gig, she was everywhere. My gran said you'd swear the Pope (the last one) had come back to life and made another visit, the way no-one would talk about anything else. Gran says some of the money's gone missing and what about that flash new apartment by the sea, but Mum says that's just rumour.

So here she is, the real thing, in a vampy scarlet kimono that clashes with her hair, waiting for me to swallow my nerves and say something.

She has her own ideas about why I'm here. 'Have you done cleaning work before?' I nod. 'I'm a student.' It's nearly true. I'm doing my Leaving this year.

'Come in.' You don't realise, on TV, not even when you hear her sugary voice, how tiny she is. Like a doll. How easily she might shatter. If she was to fall out a window, say. This close to her, I'm raw as bone. I rattle with nerves. I can't get her out of my head since all the fuss. I dream crashes and flames, her wide-eyes melting, her body twisting. I'm here to warn her, but my heart has gone on a rant of its own, won't let me speak. My hands in knots at my sides.

She doesn't notice, bangs on about where to hang my trench and leave the Nikes. She wants me in my socks on her fancy floors. Doesn't ask my name. The apartment is nothing to buzz about, but the sitting room is a surprise. It's L-shaped, a glass-walled bowl of light. The sea broods outside, flat and unimpressed.

She offers me gloves to work in – not the Marigolds Mum uses, but latex. Like *CSI*. She watches me lug the hoover out and set off across the tiles in the hall, then disappears into the ensuite, satisfied.

There's a knock at the front door. I leave the hoover running and open it. The girl out there is flushed, breathless. Upset-looking.

'Very sorry for late . . .'

'We changed our minds,' I interrupt. 'We'll do it ourselves today.' Dad gave me fifty yoyos before his latest business trip. Conscience money. I fish it out of my pocket and hand it over. 'Here.' I don't know what people get paid for cleaning, but I'd work a whole day in Copyfast for that.

She's confused. 'But, the agency –'

'It's okay. Really.' I shut the door, get back to hoovering. I didn't want that money. I want nothing from him, ever again.

' . . . there's no need to go in there.' She interrupts my little dream, blocking the door into the study. She's morphed into a businesswoman, skirt a little tight at the hips, tiny feet arched into Manolos. Hair dragged into a knot at the back of her head. 'You can do the bedroom now.'

Where it all happens. Her perfume makes me gag. I hear Mum's voice in my head, telling me to take out those dishes; pick the kimono up off the floor; hang it up. The wardrobe is crammed with frothy, useless things. A few men's suits at the back. Don't think about what happens in the bed. Tweak duvet, punch pillows. Kick a lacy string into a corner of the wardrobe. I'm not touching that. Slide the door shut.

In the shiny ensuite I remember one of those wife-swap programmes. We used to think they're hilarious. One woman made her kids scrub the loo with a toothbrush. Her's is electric. I've heard about wrecked clothes and cars, people who crap on carpets. All she'd do would be pay someone else, someone like me, to fix it.

I want to do something she'll remember.

I'm in the kitchen, wiping down the surfaces when she squints in at me through the hatch. I see a guillotine in my head. Women knitting.

'I have to run down to my car. I won't be long.' The bow of her mouth works when she talks, but her forehead doesn't crease.

Botox. She must.

The door closes behind her. I wait to hear the heavy firedoors, the ping of the lift. Slip into the study. The tiny icon of her e-mail beckons. One click and it's open. New message: 'Family News!!!'

It's one of those circulars: Little Sophie, whoever she is, has won a zillion medals for music; Conor is top of his class; Niall is a Vee Pee.

My fingers come alive on the keyboard: 'Isn't it great to hear about Mary's perfect children and her perfect life . . . Bet you've heard about mine :-) But guess what, the botox stare has begun and I might have overdone the sunbed thing, lol.'

There's a stack of bills beside me and – score! A letter from that charity: ' . . . reasonable explanation . . . account for . . . shortfall . . .' The phone rings. The answering machine clicks on. Leave a message.

Beep.

'If you're there, pick up.'

I nearly do what he says, out of habit. But I don't.

'I'll be back tonight,' he says. 'I miss you. I haven't slept since I left.'

Beep.

That makes two of us, dude. Three, if you count my mother.

Mum couldn't have any more babies after me. A messy birth, a hysterectomy. 'It wouldn't happen now,' she says.

Turns out he wanted more children, other children, all along.

Now we have to sell our house, so they can divide the money. 'When you go to college,' Mum says, 'there'll be no reason to keep it.' Her voice has a new beat, like she has to get things out through her mouth before her mind slams shut.

'I found a man and made him leave his family we've bought a brand-new apartment it's savage :-)'

Gran says fight but Mum says it's too late. She says you can't fight a baby. We'll have to sell our house in the end, because he needs – they need – a place too. She'd as soon be done with it, be free of him, start over.

Mum says don't worry, we'll find somewhere; we just have to downsize, get rid of stuff we don't need. She says what harm. She says my life will change anyway, when I go to college. Gran says she'd like to kill him. Mum says not in front of Angie, Ma, he's still her father.

They all say it has nothing to do with me. What the fuck does that mean? It has everything to do with me. It's my family that's wrecked. That's my home that's gone up for sale, that people are trekking through right now, looking through our stuff, while Mum's at work. I'm meant to be at my friend Ciara's, studying for our mocks.

He says we should get enough to buy a place somewhere in the area but we all know that's a lie. Mum's looking in the country. Not the pretty country of lambs and daffodils, but miles and miles of houses and a non-existent bus and no one we know.

Cleaning? I've done my share of it these last few weeks, clearing things out and taking them to the WaWa if they're halfway decent, to the dump if they're not. No matter what Mum says I've caught her crying over things like my TY projects and a painting I did in second class, saying she can't, she just can't, throw it all away.

I'm harder than she is. I bin stuff without looking.

I hear the lift, the firedoors. Hurry. 'His wife will be out on her ear but what harm?' I stand up, still typing.

'By the way, those rumours about the missing money are true.'

Her key in the lock.

Go to: Contacts. My fingers dance the keystrokes. Select All. Copy. Paste.

She's behind me.

'What are you doing?'

Send.

THE BARBER OF BARCELONA

by Colm Tóibín

ARTICLE 13

1. Everyone has the right to freedom of movement and residence within the borders of each state.

2. Everyone has the right to leave any country, including their own, and to return to their country.

During the day Malik made sure that the floor was swept at all times, he supplied fresh towels and he went on errands as he was told. And when the shop closed every night and the last customer was brushed clean, he was given lessons in how to cut hair. There were always willing victims who wanted a free haircut or some others who seemed to enjoy the company and the attention. The client watched in the mirror as Malik was shown how to change the head on an electric razor and how, once it was turned on, to apply the blade slowly, evenly, carefully, starting at the base of the hairline and then going in hard and close, and moving it upwards in a single gesture.

Confidence, that was the main thing, he was told, and he must not mind if he seemed to be hurting the client. 'They can take it, the skull is hard,' he was told. 'Now get the razor right in. Right in. And then up.'

But he could never manage to make it move, or if he did it was with a sudden jerk which caused the client to roar out in pain or shock or laughter. This, in turn, caused all the boys who were getting ready to leave to shout advice at Malik and warnings and gentle insults at whoever was sitting in the chair.

Sometimes he watched the barbers who had real experience working with paying customers. He noticed how they seemed to move easily from studied skill with the blade and the scissors to a sort of nonchalance as the client appeared to relax. He tried to seem confident himself but it never lasted long, he simply could not get the blade to move upwards; often it would grind against the back of the customer's head as though he was trying to cut an opening rather than give a haircut. And the more instruction he was given and the more attentive the audience, the more awkward Malik became.

At first he wondered if everyone had taken so long to learn

but now he knew that all of them thought he was slow. And that made a difference to how they treated him during the day. He wondered if it was also beginning to affect how the boys in the room reacted to him at night.

Baldy, the boss who came each evening to collect the cash, seemed too busy and preoccupied to notice what was happening. But it would just be a matter of time, Malik thought, before Baldy stopped to watch the new boy. Malik was on half-pay with no tips while he was training and this barely paid for his food and his lodgings and his laundry. As the weeks went by he began to dread the torment at the end of the day, the fierce current of the electric razor in his hand, the resentful eyes in the mirror of the man who had come to have his hair cut by the novice.

He knew that some of the boys disliked his sullenness, his silence. He kept his eyes down as he worked at keeping the place clean during the day and tried to do everything he was asked quickly and perfectly without getting in the way. Even when they were not busy they did not notice him much, or talk to him. When the shop closed, however, and he was being given instructions, they noticed him too much, openly enjoying his ineptitude and his victims' consternation, or shaking their heads in exasperation and taking over from him before he did too much damage.

He did not move beyond the street and he liked how gradually he was becoming known as he made his way to the small supermarket on the next block to buy milk or soft drinks or tea. He enjoyed being greeted and saluted. And there were other things too which made him feel comfortable. Even though eight of them shared the room, for example, he learned that he would not need to lock his suitcase, he was assured that no one would touch it. And that had proved to be true. Even one night, when one of the others wanted to move it for a moment, he came and asked permission. Slowly, he learned that they all kept money and photographs and other private things in their cases, fully confident that no one would go near them.

He noticed too that each of them had something special, a camera, a walkman, a mobile phone, a DVD player, which set them apart and that they lent out as a special favour, or at particular times. Only Mahmood owned nothing. Mahmood worked hard and spent no money because he wanted desperately to go home. Some of the others, he told Malik, spent half their earnings on phone calls to Pakistan. He had never called his wife once, he said, not even for a second. He would not waste the money and it only made him sad.

Each morning, except Saturday and Sunday, Mahmood left early to deliver butano. He carried the heavy bottles of gas up narrow staircases. And then in the afternoons he took care of all the laundry in the house, leaving clothes clean and folded on each bed, never making a mistake. And in the evening he cooked, charging less than even the cheapest restaurant.

Malik liked Mahmood from the beginning and liked having his clothes washed by someone he knew, and laid on his bed as though he were equal to the others. He also liked the food Mahmood cooked. But more than anything he was intrigued at how single-minded Mahmood was, how determined he was to go home.

Malik looked forward to the quiet time when everyone was asleep and he was woken by some stray noise. He lay there listening to the rest of them breathing in the dark, or snoring softly. On nights like this he thought that, despite the trials of training to be a barber, he was glad to be in Barcelona, happy to be among strangers and away from everyone he knew.

Baldy had told him when he arrived that he would have one day a week free but he had not mentioned which day. Since he did not want to attract Baldy's attention, Malik had not, in the first weeks, approached him about it. It was only when Super, who ran the supermarket, asked him he began to consider what he should do. In his break, he often went and sat beside Super at the cash register, enjoying how much Super seemed to know about the street and its inhabitants.

It was Super who warned him not to wander in the city. The locals were not the problem, Super said, and not even the drunken tourists. It was the police you had to be careful of. In this street and the few around it, Super assured him, they would only stop blacks, but in other streets they could easily mistake you for a Moroccan.

One day as Malik and Super observed Mahmood banging a piece of metal against the butano cylinder to let the neighbours know he was in the street, Malik told Super how great it was that Mahmood would have plenty of money when he went home because he worked so hard. Super listened and said nothing for a moment.

'No, he won't have a penny when he goes home,' Super said. 'Not a penny. They did all the paperwork for him and got him his visa and paid his fare. He is saving to pay them back so he can go.'

'Pay who back?'

'The same people who paid for you,' Super said.

Super worked alone in the supermarket and he did not have a day off. It struck Malik that Super needed an assistant, someone he could trust, someone who knew the street too and would work long hours. As he was making little progress as a barber, Malik began to consider how he might mention to Super that he would be good at stacking the merchandise and keeping the supermarket clean, that he already knew how to use the cash register.

As soon as he spoke, however, Super told him to put the idea out of his mind and advised him not to mention it to Baldy.

'It was they who brought you here,' Super said. 'You can't just move because you want to.'

At night as the others slept, Malik lay in the dark with his hands behind his head thinking of the vast city which lay around him, its night sounds seeping in. He had learned some words of the language and wondered how he might learn more. Even if he never became a barber, he thought, they would always need someone to sweep and clean. He would never go too far beyond these few streets, he was sure, but he relished the idea that other, different people lived in the city, people whom he would never meet or even see. Maybe in a while he would try just the next street. He imagined taking one street at a time, just as he imagined learning a few words every day. And maybe after a month or so, he would ask Baldy if he could have a day off, or perhaps he would ask to have two half days instead, then he would not be missed as much. It was not too bad, he thought, as he curled up in the warm bed and waited for sleep to return.

'TODAY THEY ARE NAILING THIS TERRORIST'

by Gary Mitchell

ARTICLE 14

Everyone has the right to seek
and to enjoy in other countries
asylum from persecution. This
right may not be invoked in
the case of prosecutions genuinely
arising from non-political
crimes or from acts contrary
to the purposes and principles
of the United Nations.

'ISENHEIM'

Isenheim, Robert Ballagh

'You can't nail a man to a wire fence.'

'No talking, no questions, just bring the hammer and nails.' I didn't know why Blooter was angry with me, I was just trying to help. He didn't let the door close behind him so I knew he wanted to leave immediately.

'I've been thinking about it all day,' I stalled. 'Even if you hammer the nail through his palm and tap it until it's bent around the wire, you would still have to hammer it back into his hand through the fence again because nails need something to hold them.' I didn't get to offer my idea about the piece of wood because Blooter interrupted me.

'Didn't I say shut the fuck up?'

'No. You said no talking.'

'Well, do it then.'

I didn't speak on the way out of the house. I just lifted the hammer and pushed some nails into my pocket. I paused to try to think of a better way of carrying nails but Blooter was glaring at me and I could smell the alcohol. Blooter's a nasty drunk.

I didn't speak on the way to the car, or in the car, or when we arrived at the alleyway. I just breathed in the fumes and wondered if anybody had ever got drunk just by sitting next to someone who had drink on their breath.

That was probably the longest I had been silent since the day I left school a couple of years ago. When I left that day I was afraid to speak in case I woke myself up and discovered I was still in primary school and had to do it all over again but of course things like that can't really happen.

I was holding the hammer, still speechless, when they dragged the 'guilty' man out through the back doors of the van. Clumsily, one of the men lost his grip and allowed the guilty man's left shoulder to hit the ground. It was even clumsier of the man carrying him by the leg to step on him and then kick him. It was then that I started to wish I could wake up, even if it did mean I had to go through secondary school again.

'Why are we nailing this man to the fence?'

'He's a terrorist. Not one of our terrorists. Worse. Like those people who crash planes into buildings or one of those terrorists who runs into crowds of innocent people and blow themselves up. He's one of them.'

'If he did them things how come he's not dead?'

'You ask too many questions. Remember this, you're a soldier, you don't ask questions, you follow orders.'

'If I'm a soldier give me a gun and I'll shoot the bastard.'

'You're not that kind of soldier.'

I watched Blooter smile and look away from me. I followed his eyes and we watched them drag the man I had to nail into the alleyway. I noticed a small wooden fence at the entrance and thought for a moment if I could nail his hands to that or if it would be too near to the ground.

Why can't someone print a guidebook for things like this? I mean, if you had to hang a person then it would be obvious there is a height requirement so that the man being hanged has enough room to fall the length of the rope without his feet reaching the ground so that the rope can strangle him properly, but when you are nailing a person to a fence, is it wrong if his legs are touching the ground or even sitting on the ground?

I thought about asking Blooter this question but then I remembered the last time Blooter was pissed off with me asking too many questions and how he reacted so badly.

The guilty man started screaming and moaning and begging for mercy and all this was accompanied by thuds and smacks and grunts. I tried to block out whatever was happening to him and think of something else. Blooter took his cigarettes out and handed me one. I wasn't sure if this was giving me permission to speak again or not. I took the cigarette but when I opened my mouth to put it in words just suddenly began to jump out.

'If I have to nail this man to a fence then I have the right to ask a few questions, so I do.'

That wiped the smile off Blooter's face; a fact highlighted by the way he lit his cigarette and kept the lighter lit so close to his mouth. Then he motioned it toward me and the light went out. I took the lighter and he grabbed my hand, not in a gay way but in a father to son sort of way. Where the father is a member of a vigilante-style paramilitary cell who vouched for his son to gain access even though he wasn't related to him at all. There was nothing fatherly about it actually except maybe the fact that he was a lot stronger and taller and held my arm easily and long enough to whisper his entire explanation as though warning a small child.

'This is all you need to know. This bastard left his country and came to our country because his country has the death penalty and he would be killed but here in our country we don't have the death penalty so he won't be killed. Instead he will be able to settle down here and claim all the benefits of the day. Well, today, you and I are going to explain to him why he shouldn't do a thing like that.'

'Why did he pick our country?'

'I told you. We don't have the death penalty.'

'I know but,' I don't know why I paused but I seemed to become more nervous by the second. 'How stupid would you have to be to run away from your country and end up in Northern Ireland?'

'Hey, we're ready for you,' a voice insisted from the alleyway where the screaming had stopped. I watched Blooter finish his cigarette and throw it on the ground. He stamped on it angrily but his eyes never left mine.

'Don't let me down here wee man. I'm counting on you.'

'You haven't answered all my questions yet.'

An angry man appeared at the entrance to the alleyway and signalled to us that we should hurry up. Blooter sighed heavily and used his arm to steer me away from the car in the direction of the alleyway. 'Let me tell you this. Today they are nailing this terrorist bastard. Tomorrow they might start nailing people who ask too many questions about it.'

I made a mental note to myself not to turn up tomorrow.

Blooter began to force his arm into my back making me walk faster and before I could think of my next question we were there in the alleyway. I know it was wrong but I couldn't help but smile when I saw the man was already nailed to the fence. I didn't smile because I was amused; I smiled because it meant I didn't have to nail him up.

I looked at him hanging there for a moment and tried to work out why I had this terrible aching pain in my stomach. Was I feeling sorry for this man? Empathy? Sympathy? He was a different colour. He wore very different clothes and shoes and I could hear him mumbling in a very different language. I thought I was going to be sick.

'Where is it?' The four men searched me up and down.

'Where's what?'

'The sign!'

Blooter's head dropped and I thought I could hear him making a wish. I didn't know what they were talking about so I just gave them my most confident look and allowed myself a question. 'What sign?'

'Blooter, tell me this guy hasn't come all the way down here without his sign.'

I don't know how it happened but words just began to spill nervously out of my mouth. 'Why was I to bring a sign? What kind of sign? What was the sign supposed to say? What way was I supposed to make one?'

I felt Blooter's hand squeezing my arm but I couldn't help myself. 'Maybe tomorrow you should start nailing people up who don't tell other people to bring the sign.'

The punch connected with my nose and sent a shocking pain straight to my head but as I fell backwards towards the cold, wet concrete I saw the man they had nailed to the fence and he had a look of concern on his face. His blood poured from fresh wounds and began to mix with hardened blood from wounds inflicted earlier. Maybe I was seeing things but I thought he looked like he was really worried about me.

'Why didn't you stay in your own country?'

I HAVE DESIRED TO GO

by Jennifer Johnston

ARTICLE 15

1. Everyone has the right
to a nationality.

2. No one shall be arbitrarily
deprived of their nationality
nor denied the right to
change their nationality.

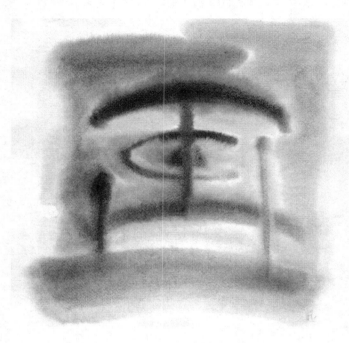

Vivienne Roche

I sit here and most of the time I look at the wall. I read, but never for long, my eyes get tired, my head droops forward, the words on the page dance in front of my eyes.

Sometimes I just sit with my eyes shut, not asleep, just staring at the insides of my eyelids.

Even in bed at night I sleep little, half an hour perhaps at a time. I am afraid of dreams. I toss and turn. I really feel the time has come for me to die. I toss and turn. I quote to myself bits and pieces I have learnt from books. Books are my home.

I have no other home.

I never have.

Of course they call this place a home but that to me is laughable. It is a storage unit: a place to keep unwanted people, old redundant people, people who are no longer needed. If you can call us people.

We have no voice.

I don't mean, of course, that we can't speak – no no no. Just that no one listens.

Even if we shouted no one would listen.

I do remember, a long time ago, I had a home; the memory flickers like a candle flame in my head.

There was a song my mother used to sing; a melancholy song which I can summon into my head from time to time.

> *I have desired to go where springs not fail*
> *To fields where flies no sharp and sided hail*
> *And a few lilies blow.*

My father wrote the music and after they had taken him away she used to sing that song.

I don't remember my father, only the few things I have been

told about him. His music is here though, songs to be sung, short pieces to be played on the piano. I, alas, do not have the skills.

> *And I have asked to be*
> *Where no storms come*
> *Where the green swell is in the heavens dumb*
> *And out of the swing of the sea.*

I was only three when they took him away and my brother Max with him.

I dream of their shadows, my father tall, Max, twelve, with a loud voice and sparking eyes.

I presumed always that when my mother sang that song that she wanted to go where they had gone, be with them. I would have liked that too. Where springs not fail. Home.

We had no home after my father was taken.

We lived in the darkness of other people's homes.

They were kind, but sombre.

I did not play with the other children, for fear.

For fear of what? I asked my mother.

She shook her head. She pressed her finger to her lips.

For fear.

I have no fear, I said to her. I want to go out and play. What is fear? She pulled me against her, wrapped her arms around me, held me so close to her beating heart that I felt it to be my heart pounding.

That is fear, she whispered, my heart beats like that because it is full of fear.

And sadness.

What is sadness? It is what I feel, she said, when I think of Max and Papa. It is what I feel when I consider how we have to live, in other people's shadowy places. It is what I feel when I think about what may happen tomorrow . . .

I was quiet then.

At that moment I did not want to ask her any more stupid questions.

But the questions crept and crept back into my mind like tiny animals, nibbling and devouring my thoughts. Questions that I knew I could not ask, questions that I knew she would not answer.

She taught me to read books and to add up numbers and subtract and multiply.

No point, she said, in you growing up without knowledge. You will find knowledge in the books, dear child. All the knowledge of the world is there and you can find it out for yourself when I am gone.

Why will you go, Mama? Why will you leave me? She shook her head.

She looked angry.

Everyone has to go sometime. That is a truth.

What will I do without you?

How do I know. Live. I hope you will be able to live.

One day she went out to get some messages. It was a bright day. The sun was shining and even the dark corners seemed full of light. I longed to go with her, I longed to feel the sun on my pale face, to feel the breeze touching my body with its fingers. I begged her to let me go with her. She shook her head. Once more she pressed her finger against her lips. Her scarf was black and green.

One day, she said, and left the room.

That was the end.

I never saw her face or heard her voice again.

They had taken her.
I suppose.
We never knew for sure.
We could only suppose.
I was six.
I could read.
I could add up and multiply.
I could sing the song my mother used to sing.

> *I have desired to go where springs not fail*
> *To fields where flies no sharp and sided hail*
> *And a few lilies blow.*
> *That will be my home.*

RIGHT OF PASSAGE

by Éilís Ní Dhuibhne

ARTICLE 16

1. Men and women of full age, without any limitation due to race, nationality or religion, have the right to marry and to found a family. They are entitled to equal rights as to marriage, during marriage and at its dissolution.

2. Marriage shall be entered into only with the free and full consent of the intending spouses.

3. The family is the natural and fundamental group unit of society and is entitled to protection by society and the State.

Arrivals. The door slides back like a curtain on a stage to reveal the travellers, with their bags and trolleys. Funny hats. Or power suits. Some faces smile, prepared to meet the faces they will meet. Some faces are surprised, some impatient. Nobody's waiting for them. Fiona could never be bored imagining the stories of the people who flow across that threshold. Out of the luggage area and into Ireland.

Soon, her husband will walk through the gate straight into her arms. He landed twelve minutes ago. She pictured him coming down the steps from the plane, his face lifting to the pleasure of fresh air. His feet have already touched Irish ground – at least, an Irish apron. Now he's probably pushing his way along the long, narrow passage that leads to the passport cubicle. Then the escalator to the luggage carousels. How long he'll be in there is anybody's guess.

After half an hour Fiona stops studying the incoming passengers. She couldn't care less now about their stories. That's a game for when you're happy. Now the only story that interests her is her own. Her eyes are fixed on the gate. It opens and closes. Opens and closes. Each opening is a squeezing of her heart and each closing a disappointment of escalating bitterness.

A few facts about Fiona, Max. The situation.

Forename: Fiona. Surname: Murphy. Date of birth: 1975. Sex: F. Nationality: Irish. Place of Birth: Dublin. Visas: Kerana, Nigeria, Kenya, India, USA, China.

Forename: Max. Surname: Ketera. Date of birth: 1980. Nationality: Keranian. Place of birth: Kerana. Sex: M. Visa: Germany.

His skin is black. It doesn't spell that out on his passport even though that's the key factor when it comes to crossing national borders. And Fiona is white; that is not mentioned on her passport either, while the colour of her eyes and the shape of her face are specified. Passports don't tell you much.

Such as, that Fiona is smart and attractive. Even now, when her belly juts before her like the bonnet of a car. She steers from above, behind the windscreen of her spectacles. 'I've changed my name,' she says. 'Meet Volkswagen Murphy.' She says this to Max, and to people in the coronary unit where she works as a staff nurse and where most of the patients are in love with her. Fiona, they call. Fiona, have you got a minute, love. Fiona is really good, they say, loudly, to their visitors, so that everyone, especially the nurses they don't like, can hear. Fiona is an angel.

Some of the juniors call her Hitler behind her back.

But nobody calls her Volkswagen. Not even Max, who is usually fond of a joke.

She met Max when she went to Africa on voluntary service overseas two years ago. Most of her friends had married. All of a sudden it was nothing but weddings. The weddings were sparkling affairs, but married life is exhausting. You can only get a house about sixty miles from where you work so you've much less time with your partner than you had before – marriage is a hobby for weekends. And the children! As soon as they're born you start wishing they'd grow up and leave home. The crèche at six in the morning. The expense. A nightmare. But the funny thing is, everyone went on marrying anyway. There was no stopping them.

Fiona decided it was not for her. Simultaneously, she decided the time had come for some sort of great change. A new continent seemed desirable.

And there in Africa: Max. She fell in love. They married. Max is a proper husband, not some sort of consolation prize for the older woman.

Handsome, educated, with a visa to study in Germany. A scholarship – he's on the last leg of a PhD in engineering in Bayreuth. And he loves music and plays the piano. A serious instrument. Actually, they share an interest in opera. Max is trying to get tickets for *The Ring* in August. (Almost impossible, but he has contacts.) So he isn't after her money or EU status, nothing like that. Anyway, getting married was her idea – it was perfectly okay with Max.

They married six months ago, when she was already pregnant. Then she had to return to her job in Dublin, and he to Bayreuth. They were to meet at weekends. But she had high blood pressure; the doctor warned her not to travel. Max has not come over until now. The scholarship doesn't stretch far, and he's busy, trying to finish his thesis. They e-mail, they Skype, she's not worried about his commitment. They're married after all.

That is, in Africa, they are married.

Not in Ireland. In Ireland, some foreign marriages are valid and some are not, and theirs falls into the latter category. That's what they told her when she rang to ask how Max could go about applying for Irish citizenship when he'd finished the PhD.

'It's complicated,' the young man had said, hesitantly, as if he was sorry about the laws of the land he served.

'But I thought if you were married to an Irish citizen, you were entitled to Irish citizenship?' She was still able to be indignant.

'That's right,' he said. 'It will probably be okay.' There was a pause. 'Write to us.' During the pause her spirits sank. When a kind young civil servant tells you he is sure it will probably be okay and pauses it means he knows it is probably going to be a disaster but he hasn't the heart to break the bad news to you.

That he'll send in the post.

'The marriage contracted abroad is not valid in this jurisdiction.'

Max was like the boy in the Civil Service.

'We can marry here,' he said. Meaning in Germany.

He asked somebody. Yes. They could. They would have to apply for permission. Wait. Then, if the application were successful, Fiona would have to be resident in the country for three months. Then they could marry. And it would probably be valid.

If all went well. (Max left out some bits; it was so complicated.)

She couldn't do it. Her job, her blood pressure. Maybe if they'd had pots of money she could have resigned. Taken the boat and train to Germany.

If you have pots of money, you can find the ways around the law, and marry whoever you like wherever you like.

If you don't, you have to stick to the rules.

Hours pass.

The mobile rings.

'I am in Clobber Eel.'

'Clobber Eel?'

A stranger takes the phone. A flat Garda voice says these two words: Clover Hill.

Then Max is back on the line.

'They're keeping me overnight and deporting me in the morning.'

He doesn't sound all that worried.

He's not in a cell, but a grey room with a table and two chairs, like those rooms they have for interrogating suspects in detective dramas on TV. He looks relaxed. But it may be just his clothes that make him look like that. Jeans and a red hoodie. Trainers. The door is locked behind them, and there is a guard in the room.

When she sees him, she realises he is the only person she wants to be with. Everyone else is a waste of her time. Her friends, her patients. A waste of time.

They kiss. There is no law against that, apparently.

And then

'Fucking eejit.'

Is what she says.

Why did he believe the marriage was valid? Why did he believe his German study visa would grant him automatic entry to Ireland? Did he ever check anything? Did he know his arse from his elbow? Did she have to investigate everything, make all the phone calls, learn the law of three countries, as well as have the bloody baby?

Max doesn't defend himself. Or remind her that the marriage was her idea in the first place. He listens patiently while she wastes the precious half hour, giving out.

The guard on duty expresses no surprise. He's used to this. It won't stop him wanting to marry either. He's already engaged to a girl from Cork. Which is okay. You're allowed to marry them.

'It will be okay,' Max says, on the phone, the next day. 'I will sort it out, do not worry.'

That's a thing men say to keep women calm. It will be okay. They'd say that if you were jumping off a sinking ship into the freezing ocean, with a suitcase in your hand and a baby in a sling around your neck. You have to wonder why anybody wants to marry such people.

❖

She is in Holles Street.

Nothing is on her mind now. Except the pain and the fear . . . It is okay, they keep reassuring her when she asks. Everything is fine. The pain comes and goes and comes and goes. Astonishing how awful it is. It is not like that clever saying, like shitting a pumpkin. It's like nothing on earth except itself.

A hundred years pass.

'Hubby,' the nurse says, with a big smile.

Hubby.

They talk like that here. Not like coronary where mostly you speak ordinary English.

The midwife rushes over and sticks something into Fiona. Her fingers.

She takes them out again, wags them in the air, triumphantly.

'We're nearly there!'

Then Max appears, above her. He seems to have floated down from the ceiling.

This time he's in a suit, white shirt, red and blue striped tie. She can't see his feet.

He kisses her.

'Everything will be okay,' he's laughing.

A civil servant in Germany said his visa should be valid for visiting another EU country. Just go back. Try again. He looked carefully at Max. Wear a suit, he said. Do not wear blue jeans. He looked down. Or trainers.

He can stay for three days. For now 'it's okay', he says, leaving out some bits, as she is pulled under a crashing wave of pain.

'And great news!'

He pulls something out of his pocket. He waves two bits of paper in the air. They are like little wings.

'I got them! I got them!'

Her heart leaps. Hope bounces into the room.

Tickets for Wagner. For *Tristan and Isolde*, not for *The Ring*.

Fiona shakes her head, as much as you can shake a head when you're supine.

Only a man, only the kind of man she would go and fall in love with, could think of Wagner at a time like this. Unbelievable.

But she still wants to be his lawful wedded wife.

Soon after that, a new sort of pain begins.

And soon after that, the gate opens.

A head comes out. Followed by a small thin body.

A new face stares at the waiting faces. A new mouth opens. And screams so loud you'd think the windows of the hospital would shatter and the glass fly out like a thousand silver stars all over the whispering streets of Dublin.

A HOME OF MY OWN

by Maeve Binchy

ARTICLE 17

1. Everyone has a right to own property alone as well as in association with others.

2. No one shall be arbitrarily deprived of his property.

John O'Brien was born in 1980. He was the first child of Mary and Jack O'Brien, he was born in a pub because Mary had got the dates all wrong and said that the baby couldn't be due for weeks yet.

She was in a pub when John arrived because otherwise she wouldn't have been with Jack. He was a man who liked being in the pub. And even more so after his son was born. He said it would destroy a man's head listening to those bellows of lungs.

But soon Dublin pubs weren't far enough from the baby's screams, so Jack O'Brien went to England.

Mary O'Brien's face was set and hard and disappointed-looking all through John's school days.

The only thing that softened those hard times was when her son did well at school. So John worked hard at his books.

It meant that he didn't go out playing games with the other lads, he didn't kick a ball around behind the school. He had no money to go to the cinema on a Saturday, instead he had a job in a garage.

His friends nagged at him, but he was firm.

'I can't lads, I just can't, she's on her own you see, my Dad did a runner, she's not strong. She can't earn much, the only hope is me.'

'It's not much of a life,' said John's friend Dekko.

'It'll get better,' John said cheerfully.

It got a bit better. Not a lot better but a bit. John didn't get the scholarships he had hoped for, so his mother's face was set in further lines of sadness. But he did get a job in a newsagents and it worked out very well for him. He suggested that they do newspaper deliveries and he also stood at bus-stops and DART stations until he found the perfect selling place.

Mr Kelly was very pleased with him. Then Mr Kelly's

daughter Orla came home from the training college where she was studying to be a teacher and she and John O'Brien fell in love. And that was wonderful altogether.

John's mother was not entirely pleased with this state of affairs, but she hid her panic that her only son might leave the nest.

But he had lived with her for long enough to read the signs. The night before he asked Orla to marry him, he told his mother that he was saving for a deposit on a house. And they would all move in as soon as he got one.

'You can't have your old mother to live with you,' she said, hardly daring to hope.

'I'm not moving without you,' John said.

'Then we hope she'll say yes,' his mother said with the first smile in a long time.

Orla said yes, her father said he was delighted and so a date was fixed, and the young couple went looking for a house. John's parents had never owned the house they lived in, nor had his grandparents. He was the first to become a homeowner. It meant safety, security, rising in the world and a place where his mother would always be welcome.

They found the perfect place; it was in a small estate and was cheaper than any of the other houses they had seen. There was a downstairs room which would be perfect for his mother, all they needed to do was to put in a downstairs bathroom.

Mr Kelly said he would help with that as it showed they were a thoughtful young couple who might not abandon him either when his time came. There was no happier man in the country than John O'Brien the day they got the key to the house and he and Orla went in to inspect their new premises. They met the people next door, a worried-looking couple in their forties.

'Aren't you as brave as lions the pair of you?' he said admiringly.

'Why?' John began to worry, was there something he didn't know?

'We're selling up and getting out,' said the neighbour. 'And here you two are full of hope and plans.'

'Well?' John was at a loss.

'"Settled" they call them but there's nothing settled about that lot,' the neighbour looked around him fearfully as he spoke.

Still John didn't know what he was talking about. 'Tinkers, Travellers whatever you're allowed to call them these days. They're going to re-house them in this estate, everyone else is running like stags and you two are delighted to be here,' he snorted a very loud snort.

John was bewildered. 'But if they want to settle down and if they are getting houses, won't they be delighted with them?' he asked.

'That lot only want a base to go robbing from, and a garden to store their broken bicycles and machinery that doesn't work. They'll have the place full of litter, and there'll be rats running over the estate before a year is out.'

'I think you're wrong,' John said. 'They'll be so happy to have running water and electricity and maybe a chance to educate their children.'

Orla agreed. 'It's so hard on the children moving on every few weeks, they never get to catch up, it will be much better for them here.'

The neighbour shook his head and said they would be singing a different song in a year's time, and if it was all the same to them, he'd sell his house to the council and just pray that whatever kind of gang might turn up wouldn't wreck the place.

Maria and Tommy McDonagh, a couple with two children, bought the house next door. They were dark-haired, handsome people and this was their first home. They had given their caravan to Maria's sister, they said wistfully as if it had been a family dog that they wondered if they could ever live without.

John and Orla welcomed them and gave them tea. Tommy talked about his hopes that he would get a job as a mechanic in a garage. He hadn't any written qualifications but he knew all about machinery. Maria said that she was going to take the children up to the school, and Orla said she would meet her there and introduce her to people.

Orla and John explained that they were getting married next week, they were having sixty people, and if Tommy and Maria would like to come, they would be most welcome. 'People don't usually ask us to weddings,' Tommy said.

'Well, I suppose if you were on the move all the time, you mightn't have been there for it,' John said, misunderstanding what the Travellers were saying.

Then the McDonaghs left because they had a lot of work to do, they said. They had to remove the garden wall.

Remove the wall? Oh yes, they needed to do that straight away.

And what for exactly? To make room for the caravans.

But hadn't they given their caravan to Maria's sister? Oh yes, they had given away their caravan, but some of their cousins might be coming to see them next week and they wanted to be ready for them.

Maria and Tommy came to John and Orla's wedding. They left their children with their cousins, who had indeed come to see them and were parked in their garden.

The hotel manager asked Tommy if there were going to be

many of his kind coming to the wedding. Tommy said no, that he was a settled Traveller now and his neighbours had invited just them.

The manager looked relieved. 'No offence, it's just that I have to look after my property,' he said.

'No offence taken,' Tommy said in a flat sort of voice.

Orla's father didn't know that Tommy and Maria were from the Travelling community. He had just been told that they were neighbours.

'I hope that you all did the right thing buying in that estate. A few people coming into the shop tell me that the worst of the tinkers are establishing a kind of fortification for themselves.'

Maria and Tommy were literally unable to answer. And as they stood there wordless, Mr Kelly, the newsagent, went on. 'Nothing against them personally, as people that is. Some of them are very decent apparently, but as soon as they come into a place the price of property halves there and then. And everyone has a right to own property and not to see its value drain away in front of their eyes.'

When Orla and John came back from their honeymoon, there had been a lot of fuss on their estate. People had come and demanded that Maria and Tommy build up their wall again. It brought the whole place down, having two trailers parked in their garden and a clothes line stretched around them.

Tommy said they were doing nobody any harm, and that he didn't object to them having people to stay or putting plastic gnomes in their gardens. The neighbours thought he was being a smart ass and said plastic gnomes actually brought the prices up. And it was all very unpleasant. People came and sympathised with John and Orla, and cast withering glances at the house next door. And John and Orla couldn't make new friends because it would be disloyal to Maria and Tommy to be mates with people who called them the scum of the earth.

So when John's van wouldn't start one cold morning, he didn't like to go to any of the other houses where there might be tow ropes or jump leads. Instead, he asked Tommy, who took the whole engine to pieces and reassembled it for him working perfectly.

The night she had the miscarriage, Orla had only Maria to call on to help her, and her shoulder to weep on when it was all over.

John's mother became frightened because there were so many confrontations outside the house when the other residents complained to Tommy, and the cousins in the trailers would answer back.

'But you like Tommy and Maria,' John begged. It was no use. His mother had her view. 'You worked hard to get property son, you have a right to enjoy it,' she said over and over.

Orla's father felt the same. He would be retiring soon and intended to hand over the business to his son-in-law but not if he was still being so foolish about this whole matter of where he lived. As soon as John noticed that he was living in a tinker encampment and moved, then he could have the business.

And the sooner the better. Orla was pregnant again and nobody wanted her in any kind of situation.

It was useless trying to convince anyone that they were happy where they were. John and Orla were trapped. How to tell them? That was the problem now.

They could lie, say they needed a bigger house for the baby and for Orla's father to come and stay. But Tommy and Maria would know. Better be honest enough to tell them the truth. They would go around tomorrow night.

Next morning, Maria and Tommy came to see them. They were tired of it all. They were going to build up the wall, collect the caravan from Maria's sister and go back on the road. All they had wanted was a bit of peace and a little property to give them a sense of belonging. It hadn't worked out. Apart from meeting John and Orla, of course, that had been great. They would never forget them.

Orla and John stood unable to think of one sentence between them.

'You two might move on anyway,' Maria said. 'When the baby comes and if your father comes to stay. So we would have lost you anyway.' Their coast was clear now, they could leave in good faith without abandoning good neighbours and good friends.

But somehow, it didn't feel good. It felt odd and confused. All anyone wanted to do was to own a small amount of property that they had bought and paid for.

That was a human right, wasn't it? And yet it seemed to have the seeds of World War Three in it.

A lot of the sunshine had gone out of the day.

CHOOSE YOUR WOUND

by Frank McCourt

ARTICLE 18

Everyone has the right
to freedom of thought,
conscience and religion;
this right includes
freedom to change their
religion or belief, and freedom,
either alone or in community
with others and in public
or in private, to manifest
their religion or belief
in teaching, practice,
worship and observance.

Choose Your Wound, Nick Miller

With the first Angelus bell bong, our teacher, Mr O'Dea, dragged his rosary beads from his trouser pocket and rushed through the Litany of the Blessed Virgin Mary and a decade of the beads in Irish.

You could see it was pure rote, that his heart wasn't in it and he did it in case the school administrator, the Rev. Dr Cowpar or his curate, Father O'Donnell, might drop in for a little inspection.

After the Litany and the rosary he made The Speech. It was five minutes of vituperation and insult in Irish and we loved it. He told us we were the most useless confirmation class he ever had, that he saw no hope, that we'd be better off in the back streets of Liverpool where they wouldn't know a sin from a monsoon.

Oh, what's the use? he said, and sat at his desk with his face in his hands.

This allowed us to smile at one another, exchange delighted nudges.

Then one day he stood, glared at us, slammed his desk with his stick and told us he had a way of saving us.

Friday, he said, is Good Friday and here is what ye are going to do. Ye are to meditate on one of the wounds of Our Lord. Ye will think of a wounded hand or foot or side or the head itself. I will now ask ye what wound ye want.

He started with the right hand and when there were only two volunteers he roared at us that he didn't know what was wrong with us, that we had this golden opportunity to meditate on the hand that so often was raised in benediction, that hand that healed lepers the length and breadth of the Holy Land.

His eloquence moved another couple of boys to volunteer for the right hand. He said they were good boys and they'd surely get a bed in heaven. Now, he said, who wants the left hand?

No volunteers.

Well, he said, that's what I'd expect from this class, this gang of spineless laners and backstreet hooligans.

He slammed his stick on the desk again. I'll tell ye what I'm going to do now. I'm going to ask each of ye what wound ye want and then I'll assign them. Hands up for the wound in the side, the Roman lance.

Five boys were lucky enough to get the wound in the side. Then he asked how many boys would like to meditate on the head, the poor tormented head pierced by the crown of thorns.

When every hand in the room seemed to go up, he roared at the four right hand boys and the five wound-in-the-side boys that they were hypocrites and they would not have hand, act or part in the crown of thorns.

Hands up again for the poor head of Our Lord who died for us.

Now he went around the room pointing at boys, assigning feet, hands, side and, for the lucky ones, the crown of thorns.

I was one of the lucky ones and as soon as I knew my assignment I began to picture the crown on my own head. I could feel it hurting already and I must have made a face because Mr O'Dea roared at me and asked if I wasn't satisfied with the crown.

Oh, no, sir. I'm satisfied. I'm happy with the crown of thorns.

Happy? Is it happy you are?

Oh, no, sir. I have the suffering. I have the pain.

He explained meditation. We were to think only of the one wound, assigned or chosen. Think of that wound morning, noon and night. Go to a quiet place and clear our minds of filth. We were to stop thinking of food, robbing orchards, and all the rotten films at the Lyric Cinema and the Coliseum Cinema, the cowboys, the gangsters and, God help us, the dancing girls.

As soon as he said dancing girls I lost my image of the crown of thorns and dreamt of Rita Hayworth.

Mr O'Dea said that in a few days it would be Good Friday and sincere boys who wanted to go to heaven would go to one or more churches on that holy day, follow the Stations of the Cross and attend the three-hour Adoration.

Go to the chapel. Kneel there till yeer knees are numb and that will give ye some idea of the sufferings of Our Lord. A numb knee isn't much but it's a beginning.

When we returned to school after Holy Week we would sit in that classroom and write a two-hundred-word composition on our meditation. If there was any blather in our compositions we'd know what it was like to suffer at the end of a stick.

Every year in our lane the mothers discussed what was the best church to attend on Good Friday and, except for a few holdouts loyal to the Franciscans, it was agreed you couldn't get better value than the three-hour Adoration at the Jesuits. They were champions in explaining the excruciating details of each wound, the significance of each wound, the miracle and wonder of each wound. Besides, the Jesuits were the only order to lay a great lifesize cross at the top of the middle aisle outside the altar rail and on that cross, His arms spread to the world, lay Our Lord Himself.

That Good Friday one Jesuit priest after another mounted the pulpit and prayed and breathed heavily and confused anyone with a limited vocabulary. One priest after another pointed to the crucifix and said, Behold. I was only ten but I wondered why they had to be so obvious. Didn't they know that this cross with Our Lord on it was the centre of attention, that we couldn't take our eyes off it? Didn't they know that even if you wanted to dream of Rita Hayworth you'd be distracted by the tragedy before your very eyes especially when you were there to meditate on the crown of thorns? They all used words so big I began to understand why people in the lanes preferred the gentleness of the Franciscans or the roaring of the Redemptorists who terrified you with visions of hell.

At three o'clock Our Lord died and the priest told us He was taken by His mother to a tomb supplied by Joseph of Arimathea. The priest said, No, not St Joseph, husband of Mary, but another Joseph and I wondered where was St Joseph when his stepson was being crucified. You'd think he might at least offer to make a coffin, carpenter that he was.

When the last priest left the pulpit, grownups stayed at their seats and sighed and snuffled in sympathy with the figure on the cross. I moved closer to the cross and stared at the crown of thorns, hoping I might think of something to write for Mr O'Dea.

Now some grownups knelt on the floor by the cross. Some kissed one or more wounds. They prayed and wept and slavered all over the wounds. I wanted to tell them stay away from the crown of thorns, that I didn't want snot and tears all over the head of my crucified Redeemer.

But I didn't because I was only ten and, even if this was a church and we were in the middle of Good Friday, they'd tell me bugger off.

If there was a competition then for which grownups seemed to be the most pious or the most suffering it was surely Mrs Reidy who carried the day. She sold newspapers down at the corner of William Street and St Patrick's Street and spent a good bit of her money on sherry at Bowles's pub on St Joseph Street. She once gave me sixpence for helping her after a fall and I always had a soft feeling for her.

Now here she was limping up the aisle, moaning and praying, her head and body under her usual black shawl. She saw me and said, Is that yourself, Frankie McCourt? and I said it was.

Like a bat unfolding she stretched out her shawl on both sides, knelt at the foot of the cross and somehow slid all the way up till her face rested on Our Lord's.

The moaning and praying in the church stopped. We listened to Mrs Reidy sobbing and hacking over the tormented face of Our Lord. She tried to caress his head but dropped her hands when she came to the crown of thorns. One of the thorns must have hurt her because she said, Ah, Jasus.

I observed that because it was my business and I thought 'Ah, Jasus' was surely the right response under the circumstances. I also thought that if one thorn could be so painful what must it be like to have . . . to have . . . ? How many? I decided . . . thirty-three, one for each year of his life, and surely Mr O'Dea will think I'm a genius for making this discovery.

Mrs Reidy might have extended her visit on the body of Our Lord to a three-hour Adoration except that a Jesuit brother came from the sacristy and helped her to her feet. He whispered to her that she should go home now, that Our Lord would be waiting for her tomorrow and if she missed Him tomorrow He'd be back next year.

He led her down the aisle to the door of the church and I thought, If she could do it why couldn't I?

I thought He'd be longer. Grownups were always telling us how Jesus was the only man who ever lived that was exactly six feet tall and here I was, only ten, almost as tall.

I slithered to the crown of thorns and it was hard being in the neighbourhood of His face with all that stuff from tears and noses and mouths, especially the stale smell of sherry left by Mrs Reidy.

I tried to find a dry spot where I could kiss the man who had saved the world, but a hand dragged me to my feet and it was the Jesuit brother telling me to get out before he reported me to the proper authorities for committing the greatest sacrilege you could think of. I wanted to ask him why it wasn't a sacrilege for Mrs Reidy or the other grownups who had been slobbering over Our Lord, but he heaved me out on the street and then disappeared inside.

Mr O'Dea said he'd read the five best wound reports to the class. He chose my crown of thorns composition. He said it was very good, especially my discovery of the number of thorns, but there was something about my remarks, about my general attitude, my miserable cheap inquisitiveness that would someday get me in trouble. He said it was a good composition and admired the way I put myself out spending all that time in a three-hour Adoration, but there was something in my story that needed to be confessed and if I knew what was good for my eternal soul I'd go to confession at the first possible opportunity.

You never know, he said. You never know.

I was only ten but I wondered even then how a composition could be good and yet a cause of confession and I wondered, even later, if that was the beginning of my drift away from the church.

WHY ARE YOU DOING THIS?

by Dermot Bolger

ARTICLE 19

Everyone has the right
to freedom of opinions
and expression; this
right includes freedom
to hold opinions without
interference and to seek,
receive and impart information
and ideas through any media
and regardless of frontiers.

'Why are you doing this?' she said, bewildered and more than a little hurt.

'Because this is how I remember it, this is how I want it to be expressed.'

'But perhaps you remember it all wrong.' Patiently, parentally, she tried again. 'Perhaps what you write will be lies?'

'This is still how I remember it.'

'Then maybe it is best to stop remembering? What good will remembering things do? Dragging things up won't change anything. All you will do is to hurt people who have tried to rebuild their lives and yours. The past belongs to the past.'

'My past, as I remember it, belongs to me and nobody else.'

'But, don't you see, nobody will believe you if you say these things.'

'I don't care.'

'I mean that nobody will want to believe you and then you'll just feel worse. It's just too inconvenient for people to accept that such things went on. Can't you recognise this and draw a line under it, like the rest of us? I'm not admitting that the things you claim happened did happen, but, just supposing they did, what will be gained by going on about them now?'

'I have the right to do so.'

'What right? The right to be awkward and ungrateful? The right to drag us back into the mess that any sane person would want to forget? It's not love that holds a society together, it's collective amnesia. That is how we muddle by. Maybe it's time you started believing in something different. There are so many better beliefs that will help you forget. Before you started getting these notions you were content with what you now have. You're safe in a place where such people can never again touch you. You need to stay safe by keeping your head down.'

'I need to be heard.'

'I'm telling you they won't listen. You'll gain nothing and lose your anonymity. Life has moved on, people will simply say that you remember it wrong. You go on about your rights, but what gives you the right to tear this family apart? How do you think we're going to be able to live together afterwards, as a society, as a people? You will have made your point, made yourself a martyr, but what about the rest of us? If you have a right to remember, then surely we have a right to forget. Do you honestly think that when we are finished screaming those old justifications we will understand each other any better? Do you think your one-person truth commission will resolve anything that could not just be papered over? Do you honestly think the world will be better for old wounds being dragged up? You were not the only victim, you know, this is not all about you.'

'I am the only one I can speak for.'

'Maybe the others don't want their stories told, maybe your words will make them victims twice over. These are consequences you must consider.'

'I simply cannot pretend that bad things never happened.'

'Bad things happen in every society, some societies are just better at hiding bad things than others. Mistakes occurred, nobody is denying that. Mistakes occurred because we didn't always possess names for things, we trusted authority too much or feared authority too much, we didn't always grasp the consequences of actions, we were too busy trying to simply survive. What gives you the right to suddenly be our judge and jury? Just be warned that when you find us all guilty, you may find yourself guilty too. That's the problem about looking back – you find that we all played some small part in the cover up, because this is what we do to survive when we find ourselves in certain places at certain times. We're only human, we're not saints or martyrs. We saw what we saw and chose to turn a blind eye because we could change nothing. We buried our heads because we had people to protect: children and infirm dependants who relied on us. You call that compromise but I call it life. When the men came at night they were always going to take away certain types. I alone could not stand up to them. I didn't like what I saw, but I held my silence, I did not step forward, because if I did so you would have starved. You were too young to have to make such choices. I protected you as best I could, even if I could not protect you from people whom I should not have trusted. Your words won't hurt those people now, because they are beyond hurt, but they will hurt me by making the world see me as a collaborator, when all I wanted was that my family would survive.'

'I still want to write down what I know.'

'Why sit on your high horse and judge us?'

'Because I remember what I remember. Because I believe that I have the right to be a jumped up little bastard, a black sheep, a grating voice that nobody even listens to, who gets facts wrong but maybe gets some facts right. Maybe I can barely spell or pronounce the words I want to use. But why should only the powerful, the correct and the sanitised be heard? What about the voices of children kneecapped in lanes, of bodies shot in ditches, of some girls forced to give birth and of other unlived lives that might have blossomed wondrously had doctors not crushed their skulls in clinics? Why can't I scream my belief in Christ or scream that with God gone there is only a black void in which all the heroin on earth cannot cushion your fall? Why should I not reserve the right to feel hatred, the right to feel intimidated by the hordes that invade my streets and destroy my sense of home?

Why should I not reserve the right to lust, the right to desecrate and blaspheme and deny, the right to be annoying and at times only half-right or maybe not right at all? I reserve the right to express my views, no matter how uncomfortable they make you. I reserve the right to say and think and feel what I feel and know what I know, even if what I know turns out to be wrong.'

'Nobody is stopping you from thinking such things,' she said, 'but why must you write them down?'

'Because too many people were not allowed to write it down. Because books and letters and diaries were concealed under floorboards and burnt if found. Because new meanings were imposed on old words. Because people were imprisoned for laughing at cartoons, or for not laughing hard enough. Because audiences stood up to clap dictators until their hands were raw, each afraid to be the first to stop. Because parents were too afraid to address their children when whisperers listened everywhere, when dossiers were stoked, when neighbours informed from hunger or spite or because they needed to believe in their jailers. Because children were seized from parents to be re-branded in the outback, and schizophrenics were sterilised in the Nordic cold and no letters could be written when post was seized. Because poems were evidence, passing whispers a more precious commodity than gold or bread. Because a thought was as bad as a deed. Because daughters were too shamed to speak to mothers, because estates were ruled by thugs, because transistors needed to be hidden, because websites were blocked. Because helicopter propellers stirred up the waves as they accepted the silent weight of the disappeared, because a child died from hunger having never yet uttered a word, because too many married couples have shared beds portioned by the unspoken. Whatever small things I need to say are inconsequential compared to all the lost words, all the thoughts people needed to suppress, all the desires they did not possess a language for. I cannot fill their silence, but I will say what I need to say, although trivial in the scale of life, although awkward to some, although stupid even or fanciful or obscene. I will risk being wrong because I reserve the right to be wrong. I will scrawl it in graffiti no matter how often the wall is whitewashed. I will leave notes on margins. I know what was done to me and I will stay quiet no longer. I know what I did and I will confess my sins. I know what I desire and I will speak of my needs. I know that I have the right to not know what I truly want. I know that millions died with stories far more urgent, but my story remains my own to express.'

She shook her head, still baffled, still hurt.

'And what will you gain by this grand gesture?' she asked. 'After you have hurt us all with your truth and your lies. After no one believes you, after people turn their back? What will you have gained?'

'I will have gained a voice.'

ST MONANCE (PEER EDUCATION)

by Irvine Welsh

1. Everyone has the right to freedom of peaceful assembly and association.

2. No one may be compelled to belong to an association.

Ah wisnae chuffed aboot this rehab situ, but after bein caught rid-handed comin oot the sheltered housin complex it wis that or the jail. N gettin the fuck oot ay Leith fir a couple ay weeks would be sound: the place wis like the Marie Celeste. Sick Boy had vanished, his Ma said tae her sister's in Italy. Swanney had gone tae ground n thir wis nae sign ay Spud; the poor cunt wis probably still at Scotch Corner. As fir everybody else, ah jist wanted tae scream in thir faces, Tommy, Begbie, Keezbo, the loat ay thum: fuck pubs, fuck Hibs, fuck birds, fuck mates, aw ah care aboot is skag, so jist fuckin well gie's some fuckin peace!

It pished doon oan the drive tae the centre, a two-storey white buildin, in the middle ay fuckin naewhaire in Fife. Ah sat in the back as ma faither drove in silence, my Ma gabbin nervously in between chain smokes. When we git thaire ahm hurtin bad. Ah cannae even climb oot the back seat of the car when the old boy gets oot n opens the door. Suddenly, a sweat-inducing pulse ay terror rises in me. Ah'm shitein it.

– Ah dinnae want tae dae this!

As ah hear my Ma say something aboot a fresh start, ma faither goes, – Well, it's oot your hands now, pal.

– What gie's youse the right tae make ays?

My Ma looks at me, twistin roond in the seat wi her big doolaly eyes. – We care son, that's what gie's us the right, she shakes her heid and opens the door, musing, – Ah dinnae ken why this has happened tae us . . .

– Mibbe it's God, ah venture. – Giein ye another test, likes.

She looks at me and springs out the car, shouting at my dad. – Did ye hear um Davie! He's evil, she points back tae me in the motor, – Listen tae yersel, ya ungrateful wee –

– It's the drug talkin, Cathy, the drug, dad sais wi grim authority. Now that the Auld Girl wis kickin oaf, he could play good cop. The Auld Boy had a temper but was loathe tae lose it. The Auld Girl wis always easy going, so ma tactic wis tae get her tae play the bad fucker, which disarmed the Auld Boy's anger. But now ahm puppy-seek n runnin oot ay time.

Thir wis naewhaire roond here tae dae a runner tae. Jist some poxy village wi a few hooses, a pub, n this fuckin centre. We walk doon the gravel path tae the front door. It's exactly like the Sheltered Housing place ah tried tae screw; same magnolia waws, broon kerpit tiles, harsh lights n that omnipresent stench ay state control.

The centre director is a skinny woman wi dark, curly hair that's tied back, black-rimmed glesses n fine, delicate features. She ignores me, electin tae shake hands wi ma parents. A big, wholesome cunt wi a blonde fringe smiles at me, – I'm Len, he takes ma bag, – I'll take this tae yir room.

The Auld Man scans the doss. – Seems a no bad billet though son, he gies ma hand a squeeze. There's mist in his eyes. – Fight through it, pal, he whispers, – We believe in ye.

Skinny-Specky is blabbering oan tae my mother who's looking confused. – The essence of St Monance is a collaborative venture between two Health Boards and three Social Work Departments, the detox programme followed by client-centred individual and group counselling sessions.

– Aye . . . that's nice . . .

– The group is crucial to our philosophy. It's seen as the way to combat the peer structures on the outside that support the addict's behaviour.

– Aye . . . nice . . . cosy, she sais, lookin at the curtains.

– Well ye'll get nae bother fae him, my dad goes, turnin tae me, – Yi'll take yir chaunce here. Right?

– Right, ah say.

Ma first chance tae git the fuck oot.

– Anything tae get ye oaf the streets, away fae they losers n bams like that Spud laddie, n thon Matty. Nae ambition, he shook his heid.

– Removal from the peer environment is one of our key elements. Let the client take stock, so sayeth Skinny-Specky.

– They'll drag ye doon tae thaire level, son. Ah've see it, my Ma warns.

– That's ma mates. Ah've goat the right tae hing aboot wi who ah want.

– Thir junkies, she scowls.

– So? Thir no hermin anybody.

– The coorts saw it differently, my faither groans miserably. – Ye wir caught red-handed son, leavin thair wi that stuff. An auld woman, son. A pensioner.

Some auld minger that's gaunny be fuckin deid soon anywey . . . grassin auld cunt . . .

– Ye were better oaf hingin aboot wi Tommy n Francis, son, Ma urges. – The fitbaw, n that. Ye eywis liked the fitba.

A sudden bolt ay panic. Ah turns tae ma new hosts, – Will ah git anything here, like methadone?

– That depends, Skinny-Specky goes.

– On what? Now ah'm lookin at her like she's the only yin in the room.

Her glance is measured and unfazed. Its like she's seein me fir the first time. – On a number of things, but chiefly on how you respond. There will be on-going assessment. Take note though: we only prescribe methadone in extreme circumstances. This is about being drug-free. You'll be part of a group, a society here at St Monance, one that works, rests and plays together, and it will be tough.

Ah suspect thit that speech wis really fir ma parents. My Ma gies me a bone-crushing hug. Ma faither, noting my obvious discomfort, settles fir a weary nod. He hus tae pull her away; she's sobbin her fuckin eyes oot, makin a fuss, a drama oot ay things.

– But he's ma bairn, Davie, he'll eywis be ma bairn . . .

– C'mon now, Cathy.

– Ah'll get masel sorted oot here, Ma, you'll see, ah try n crack a smile.

Just fuckin go! Now!

Ah want tae lie doon. Ah dinnae want tae be part ay Skinny-Specky's daft wee group, her fuckin society. But nonetheless ah'm awready daydreamin aboot fawin in love wi her; me n Skinny-Specky oan a Caribbean Island wi an endless supply ay gear, procured fae her employers in the NHS. She's like one ay they sexy librarian birds thit wid be shaggable as fuck when hair tumbles doon n the T-Rex come oaf. No that shaggin wid be much oan the agenda. Shall we make love on this beach underneath the stars or fix up again?

Your turn tae cook, Skinny-Specky.

Ah git tae ma room n lie oot oan the bed, but Len-the-Fringe comes back. – Don't get too comfortable. Our induction meeting's just about to start.

Other cunts! Aw naw. – How many's here?

– We have nine clients.

He leads me doon a corridor, but as we step intae this big room, the first thing ah hear is: – RENTON, YA CUNT, then aw this laughter followed by a round ay applause. Ah cannae fuckin believe it. Thir aw here! – Fuck sakes! Youse cunts!

– Goat the fill set now, boys, Johnny Swan laughs as Len cringes.

It's like a surprise birthday perty. Swanney's wearin a fuckin tie!

There's Matty, zonked oot, and Spud shiverin, airms wrapped roond himself. – Catboy, eh sais.

And Sick Boy's slumped in a corner seat. Ah nods n sits doon beside um. – Nice place yir Auntie's goat.

Eh pills a tired smile. – Hud tae be done.

Spud asks Len aboot getting something for his cramps as Sick Boy and Swanney intro ays tae a couple ay Edinburgh boys, a biker called Seeker, whae ah ken by rep, n a shifty gadge called Mikey Forrester. Thir's a wee cunt, Ted fae Bathgate, n two Weedgie boys, thit git kent as Garbo n Skreel.

Swanney winks at me n pills oot a wee razor blade. Then he nicks the inside ay his mooth, catchin the blood in his hands, looking tae Len, whae's shitein it. – Ma stitch hus burst . . .

– The nurse isn't in . . .

– Ah'll chum um tae git cleaned up, ah quickly volunteer.

– Right . . .

Sick Boy, Matty and Spud look daggers at us as Swanney n me nash doon the hall tae the bogs. He's goat works doon his boot and we quickly cook up. He pills oaf his tie n torniquet's me. We're dabbin away at a wrap ay speed n it faws oot my hand as he slams me up and the heroin goes tae ma brain, killing aw the world's pain.

Ah sit blissed oot oan the crapper as Swanney fixes, tellin me that one ay the Weedgie boys is hudin. He retrieves the speed wrap n we finish it, even though it's the last thing ah want. He struggles tae fix his tie. – A great network ay contacts here.

When we get back Len-the-Fringe and Skinny-Specky have launched intae this spiel but nae cunt's listenin tae thum, thir aw slumped back in thir chairs. Aye, it's gaunny be awright in here. These are ma people: ahm happy tae be part ay the St Monance crew.

THE PROBLEM WITH DEMOCRACY IS THE PEOPLE

by Lara Marlowe

ARTICLE 21

1. Everyone has the right to take part in the government of his country, directly or through freely chosen representatives.

2. Everyone has the right of equal access to public service in his country.

3. The will of the people shall be the basis of the authority of government; this shall be expressed in periodic and genuine elections which shall be by universal and equal suffrage and shall be held by secret vote or by equivalent free voting procedures.

A tall Sudanese servant in a white robe and turban opened the door and led the way through the residence, gliding over Persian carpets and marble floors. Dust hung in shafts of light. Here and there, the glint of gold leaf or brass, rainbows cast by bevelled mirrors on cream-coloured walls.

The Ambassador sat in a wicker chair on the veranda. 'Hello Woodrow!' he said, rising to receive the late arrival. 'How good of you to come! Cynthia will join us later. She's suffering from one of her migraines.'

A ceiling fan whirred above them. As a clock chimed the half hour, the timer on the irrigation system kicked in. The sprinkler heads hissed and spluttered before spraying arcs of water across the lawn. The Ambassador's golden Labrador raced about, grabbing sprinkler heads in his muzzle.

'Ustez Mohamed!' Woodrow said. 'It's great to see you!' The white-haired historian set down his whiskey glass and cigar to shake the journalist's hand.

'So you two know each other,' the Ambassador said, turning to introduce silver-haired Khadija Sultan ('our neighbour, and a formidable businesswoman'), Miloud Ramadan, whom he described as a human rights lawyer, and Miloud's pregnant wife, Aliya. The young woman's thick, black eyeliner reminded Woodrow of the Cleopatra soap package.

'Woodrow has been covering the election,' the Ambassador announced. 'Tell us what you saw, Woodrow.'

'Well, the worst place was the polling station in Agouza,' Woodrow said, watching the other faces, afraid he might offend them. 'It was chaos. There were teenage girls screaming, gouging each other's faces, pulling hair. The police were bashing people with rifle butts, and I saw them break padlocks on ballot boxes. Very civilised.'

The coffee table was laden with raw almonds floating in bowls of ice water, pistachios, carrot and celery sticks, biscuits coated in sesame seeds.

Khadija Sultan reached for an almond. 'A catastrophe,' she muttered, shaking her head as she peeled the outer green flesh from the almond. 'My foreman was killed in a polling station. Can you imagine . . . a gunfight between Islamists and the President's supporters – in central Cairo! It's nearly impossible to find an honest foreman. I don't know how I'll run the factory without him.'

'My dear, try to care a little for your own country!' Mohamed scolded Khadija. The look she shot him spoke of past quarrels. 'Before the election even started, they arrested six hundred members of the Muslim Brotherhood. Almost all of them were delegates who were supposed to monitor ballot boxes. I know several of them, and I honestly believe these people were trying to play the democratic game, such as it is here. They are educated, moderate people and they know how crude the power of the state can be in a Third World country. They were sentenced to five years in prison. I cannot accept it with a good conscience.'

Woodrow slyly pulled a notebook from his jacket pocket and began taking notes. The Ambassador scowled at him.

'So Mohamed,' Khadija said. Woodrow had never heard anyone address the ageing historian and television personality without the honorific prefix *ustez*. 'You've got a soft spot for the Islamists. Just wait until they come to power. I promise it will be the end of your cuties and whiskey!'

The older man ignored her. 'I'll tell you how elections are rigged in this country,' Mohamed continued. 'There is never much of a turn-out, because people know better. At the end of the day, delegates from the President's party fill out the ballots, under police supervision, so everyone registered on the list votes. They make a dash next to each name. It's a foregone conclusion the NDP will get at least two thirds of the seats, because He has to be elected by two-thirds of the parliament, and He wants to be President forever.'

Khadija and Miloud exchanged uncomfortable glances. A waiter refilled the drinks.

But Mohamed was relentless. 'This country is suffocating. Most of the ministers have held the same posts for twenty years. Did you hear about the demonstration two weeks ago at Cairo University? They arrested fifty students. Five were sent to jail on the attorney general's orders. The other forty-five were taken to the central security camp with their families. They're being kept there without food or water, because they want to intimidate them. They have to buy food and water from the guards.'

'I hear a lot of detainees are tortured,' Woodrow remarked archly.

'Of course they are,' Mohamed replied. 'It's all of a piece. You're Pharaoh and you want to stay in power, but you need the Americans' support. So you have to hold elections. But to win the elections, you have to arrest people and torture them, humiliate them so they won't be Islamists . . . You should write about Tora prison, south of Cairo,' Mohamed said, turning to Woodrow. 'They give the prisoners female names, and force them to bugger each other.'

The more furiously Woodrow scribbled, the more Mohamed talked. Then the old man turned on Miloud.

'You're supposed to be a human rights lawyer. Why don't you denounce these abuses?'

Miloud squirmed in his vanilla-coloured suit, and Cleopatra watched his face, one hand on her pregnant tummy.

'I used to be more outspoken,' the lawyer admitted. 'I spent three months in prison. Oh, I know Mohamed. You did too. Under Nasser. It was different in those days. But then I saw the bombings and assassinations, and I suppose I thought the Islamists were the greater evil. I don't want them to come to power, because that's what will happen if we have free and fair elections. We'll end up with an Islamic republic, and there'll be no more elections. I know the regime's not worth defending. I want us to have democracy, like Europe or America. But I don't know how we get there. I've thought a lot about it, and there is no solution.'

'You're pathetic,' Mohamed said softly, and the others pretended they hadn't heard him. Then he raised his voice again. 'Ah, the problem with democracy is the people!'

'You created the fundamentalists,' Woodrow said, looking at Khadija and Miloud. In ordinary circumstances, he would not have spoken out in front of the Ambassador, but Mohamed's presence emboldened him. 'You created them, and now you have to live with them.'

Khadija shifted her bulk in her armchair. 'We are fighting terrorism, Mr American Reporter,' she intoned. 'You don't do that with the Declaration of Human Rights in one hand and the constitution in the other. You don't fight terrorism with kid gloves. You media are like the so-called human rights groups, who only care about fanatics and terrorists.'

'The government is wasting the country's time on this silly conflict,' Mohamed said. 'They have no ideology – not secularism, not democracy. They are spoiled and corrupt.'

Khadija rolled her eyes. The Ambassador's wife stood like a ghost in the doorway. 'Dinner is served,' she announced flatly. A smile of relief spread over the Ambassador's face. It was twilight, and the air had cooled. Cleopatra pulled a shawl over her shoulders.

As the guests made their way towards the dining room, the Ambassador placed a hand on Woodrow's forearm, to hold him back. 'Now Woodrow,' he said, 'you have to be careful of Mohamed. That was the whiskey talking. You know, he enjoys a special status in this country. He feels he's untouchable, but nobody takes him seriously anymore. I was at the presidential palace this week, and they really are trying. If you write these things, they'll only get discouraged. You do understand, don't you Woodrow?'

'Of course, Ambassador.'

The head waiter lit the dining room candles. When all were seated, the shrimp cocktail served and the Chassagne Montrachet poured, a non-descript man walked in and whispered in the Ambassador's ear. Woodrow recognised the political councillor.

'Election results just in,' the Ambassador announced with a cynical smile. 'The President's party has won an absolute majority. Don't worry, they've left a few seats for the Wafd and the leftists, but the president will be re-elected.'

The Ambassador raised his glass.

'To democracy!' he said.

The guests raised their glasses, looking sheepish. Surely the Ambassador mocked them?

'To democracy!' they murmured in unison, clinking their crystal glasses.

HOW DO YOU DRAFT A PLAN TO FIX A BROKEN WORLD?

by Mark O'Halloran

ARTICLE 22

Everyone, as a member
of society, has the right
to social security and
is entitled to realisation,
through national effort
and international
co-operation and in
accordance with the
organisation and
resources of each state,
of the economic,
social and cultural
rights indispensable
for their dignity and the
free development
of their personality.

1. Imagine now a man who is deprived of everyone he loves, and at the same time of his house, his habits, his clothes, in short, of everything he possesses: he will be a hollow man, reduced to suffering and needs, forgetful of dignity and restraint, for he who loses all often easily loses himself.

– *If This Is a Man* by Primo Levi (Jewish-Italian chemist, Holocaust survivor and author of memoirs, short stories, poems and novels.)

In 1945, the world was a broken place. Near the halfway point of a century that would prove to be the most savage and bloody in human history, at the end of a World War that had killed 50 million people, and in a time when the imagination of mass slaughter had reached sickening heights, it must have felt as though mankind was losing an essential part of itself, its own common humanity.

Throughout the war and in preparation for the peace that was to come, many groups and individuals had spoken up for the idea of a charter to be constituted that would stand up as a list of the basic and universal human rights. As the war came to a close, however, and in the terrible shadow of Auschwitz and the sheer depravity of the war crimes committed, those calls for a recognition of human rights as being central to international law became deafening.

It was for this reason that, after the United Nations was formally established in 1945, one of the first actions of its newly established Economic and Social Council was the convening of a Commission on Human Rights, whose job it was to draft a bill of the basic rights of man. The enormity and complexity of this task cannot be underestimated. The committee was being asked to compile a bill of rights that went beyond political dogma and religious belief, that was universal and cross-cultural, and that would be a statement of the moral rights and principles that would embody the hopes of millions of oppressed individuals. It was as if the drafters were being asked to answer the question 'what is a man?', and there were many who believed it could not be done.

However, under the chairmanship of Eleanor Roosevelt, the committee, comprising delegates from eighteen countries, realised it was a question that needed to be tackled before the notion of permanent peace, stability and security in the world could even begin to be entertained or contemplated. Under Roosevelt's heroic leadership, the drafting process took almost two years, and the resulting declaration is radical in that it represents an emphatic statement that human rights belong to everyone without distinctions as to race, sex, language or religion.

> 2. The peoples of the world are on the move. They have been given courage by the hope of freedom for which we fought in this war. Those of us who have come from the murk and mire of the battlefields know that we fought for freedom, not for one country, but for all peoples and for all the world.
>
> – Carlos Romulo (Filipino diplomat, politician, soldier, journalist and author. He led the Philippines delegation in the negotiations to draft the Universal Declaration.)

Over the drafting period, a number of events and circumstances would conspire to thwart the committee's work and progress. To begin with, there was confusion as to what the committee was actually supposed to be attempting. Some believed that, for the project to have any significance, the committee should steer away from the construction of a vague set of principles in the form of a declaration that would have no meaning in law. They believed it was the work of the committee to realise a binding covenant that would have to be ratified by the member states of the United Nations and would come with its own implementation structures and bodies. The construction of such a covenant, however, would have been an extremely arduous task, would have required drafting by teams of international law experts, and would have taken a prohibitively long time.

The more pragmatic members of the committee realised that, with the Cold War gathering and deepening, and with the US and USSR in no mood to construct such international court structures, the only achievable goal in the short term would be to use the politically favourable period of consensus on human rights to construct an acceptable declaration.

The fact that the Declaration, when it arrived sixty years ago, did not come with any machinery of implementation dismayed many, but it did have a different and unique strength. The simplicity and clarity of the Declaration seems to accord it an independent moral status in world affairs and law. On its own, the declaration has directly inspired two covenants at the UN – on Civil and Political Rights and on Economic, Social and Cultural Rights – but it also became the inspiration for a whole branch of international law. Whereas before the Second World War there were few independent instruments concerned with the realisation of human rights, since then, and with the Declaration acting as a sort of talisman to the dignity of the individual, that situation has been transformed. Its existence does not mean we live in a world at peace, or in a world where men, women and children are free from torture or exploitation, but perhaps it allows us to catch a glimpse, a very fleeting glimpse, of what such a world might look like, and allows us to believe in the inalienable dignity of each individual.

> 3. Political rights are the first condition of liberty but today the progress of scientific and industrial civilization has created economic organisations which are inflicting on politically free men intolerable servitude and that, therefore, in the future, the declaration of the rights of man must be extended to the economic and social fields.
> – Henri Laugier, April 1946 (UN Assistant Secretary-General for Social Affairs at the time of the drafting of the Declaration.)

Article 22 is the first article in the Declaration to tackle the social, economic and cultural rights of man. In the early stages of the drafting process some believed that such rights did not belong in the Declaration at all. It was believed that 'civil and political rights' took precedence over 'social and economic rights' because, according to some, the former are a prerequisite for the latter, but not vice versa. The British and Australian delegations in particular argued fiercely for the exclusion of these rights. To their thinking, the inclusion of economic and cultural rights would muddy the waters and, as the UK delegate Lord Dukeston put it, 'the world needed free men and not well-paid slaves'. But it could equally be asked: what use are civil liberties to the person if he is not protected against poverty?

As Eleanor Roosevelt herself stated, 'freedom without bread has little meaning. Freedom from want and freedom from aggression are twin freedoms that go hand in hand,' and so eventually the argument to include these 'new' or 'non-traditional' rights was won. For the first time, it was being accepted that a permanent system of security could be effective only if it had a foundation in economic and social justice. The understanding that freedom from hunger and disease as a matter of right is as essential to human dignity as freedom of expression or conscience was an important and hard-won argument. Expanding civil and political freedoms is indispensable to combating poverty, but on its own cannot remedy the chronic levels of deprivation and want that continue to blight much of humanity.

Article 22 itself came late in the drafting process and can be seen as a covering article for the articles that follow, which deal with employment, leisure, education and community. It states, in clear terms, that everyone has the right to social security, but it then goes beyond looking merely on the rights of the individual but on the rights of the individual as a member of society.

It says everyone has the right to the realisation of his social, economic and cultural rights, which are essential to the development of his personality, but that these rights can only be realised through the efforts of society and through international co-operation. In other words, by acknowledging that these rights can only be achieved through the efforts of us all, it is saying something very simple and very beautiful. It is saying we belong together.

In the words of Eleanor Roosevelt, 'I don't believe that greed and selfishness have gone out of the human race. I am quite prepared to be considerably disappointed many times . . . but I want to try for a peaceful world. The ratification of the treaty . . . I think, makes easier every step we take in the future.'

'THEY WERE TRYING TO ISOLATE ME'

by Ann Marie Hourihane

ARTICLE 23

1. Everyone has the right to work, to free choice of employment, to just and favourable conditions of work and to protection against unemployment.

2. Everyone, without any discrimination, has the right to equal pay for equal work.

3. Everyone who works has the right to just and favourable remuneration ensuring for themselves and their family an existence worthy of human dignity, and supplemented, if necessary, by other means of social protection.

4. Everyone has the right to form and to join trade unions for the protection of their interests.

And that was it, the job was mine. That was on the Friday and the following Monday I met the supervising porter at the front gate and introduced myself to him, and he introduced me round and he just basically told me roughly what the job was. He didn't even tell me really what it was, it was just: 'You'll be working round the porters.' And I got no contract, signed no contract, signed nothing, did no, no, no terms nor nothing. Never. Never signed a contract. I wasn't even vetted by the police. Which is a regulation, which is a requirement that they have to do because you could be any sort of criminal, or any sort of maniac, yeah.

And I was working there I'd say near enough to a year before they brought down this form to me to fill in. So I was probably working there about eleven months, near enough to that, before they even got me to fill in the form. So I could have been Jack the Ripper for all they knew. But that's acceptable practice anyways. That's normal. And I started in there, in a big hospital, and I worked in there and my title was Relief Shift Porter.

It was a doddle, like. You see a lot of the lads, a lot of the porters, there were a lot of porters up there, well maybe twenty porters. In my view they were overstaffed. A lot of them, a lot of the older, the senior porters – which is what they like to call themselves – went in and did about, in an eight-hour day, they worked about an hour in the whole eight hours and they sat on their backsides for the rest of the day. Watching the football and putting on bets.

I could do a whole day's work in an hour. First thing I did was take a trolley full of laundry up to the ward. Then I'd take a trolley full of dirty laundry down from the ward to the laundry. Then I'd take a trolley full of food up to one ward, and bring that trolley back down. In the afternoon I'd bring up one trolley from the laundry again. Some porters only did that. The privileged porters did just that. Unless they were stuck. The new porters did the laundry, the slop, the patients, the lot. They got the younger, newer fellas to do all the dirty work. They were like kings. Good amount of money, all the overtime.

So you're talking about a lot of money when you added in the overtime and the allowances. The basic wasn't that strong. But then when you thrung in your allowances, your overtime, your Bank Holiday allowance, your Sunday allowance, your night-shift allowance, it was high. That's where an awful lot of trouble developed.

There were twenty or twenty-two porters and a hard core of about six porters. They were referred to as the senior porters but some of them were only a wet day in the place. The management left the porters' department alone. If a young porter came into the hospital and wanted a share of the overtime, or even wanted a share of, of, what would you call it, the luxury time, the easy time, easy street, you know, you're not going to share the easy street, the senior guys . . . now when I say the senior guys, like that again it's very perceptible. Like that, as I was saying to you, it's who you know. One or two of these guys were only in the hospital for a year but because they were friends with some of the senior porters, they were classed as being senior.

So like that again, you got your privileges depending on who you were friends with. You know. So if some of the young fellas were looking for a bit of overtime, or looking to enjoy a bit of the luxury, the easy time, like us all, we all want the easy job, to be there watching television, like everyone else, you know. Then these older guys would attack these young fellas, abuse them. Call them names. If a person had a deformity, or if, if they had a disability, or if they had some sort of quirk, or mannerism. And for them being a woman was a deformity, being black was a deformity.

Give you an example. There was one fella who walked like John Travolta. Great walk. He strutted, right? He was only a young fella. He's probably out of nappies now, he hadn't experienced life at all. But all the women loved him and stuff like that. But a good worker. A good worker, nice man – but he had this walk on him. He got into fierce trouble. They'd tell everyone he was queer and they'd be plastering his private affairs all over. He had to be eliminated. His professional reputation had to be eliminated. That was the norm. It happened to many, many people. We were told people were going to work in other parts of the health service.

There were periods of stability and common sense when the head porter was out sick. Then he'd return and there'd be chaos. He ran the department through this gang of heavies. There was no training. They were doing it blindfolded. There was a lot of inconsideration, a lot of roughness with patients.

If he wasn't out sick, the head porter would go and do the post. That was the only time I'd see him. He'd come in about nine, nine-thirty, to issue a few preliminary instructions and to have a shower and doll himself up. He was the most groomed person I ever seen. He'd deliver the post round town then and be back around four. He'd be back at lunch as well for about an hour. So, back round four, just as everyone was leaving.

There was a new unit to be opened which was dependent on the porters. The porters were up in arms with this being built.

They were up in arms. In order to pacify them, the management had to have a number of meetings to try and coerce their co-operation. In the course of the meetings a commitment was given that the porters would get first call on any new jobs in the new unit. I think this is highly improper. Jobs should go to the best people.

The new unit brought in its own staff. But they couldn't get their post. At the time I was responsible for delivering the post all over the hospital. I was approached about delivering post to the new unit and I said, 'No problem, it's my job.' There was an internal convulsion, an internal rebellion against the management. Against the new unit. They came to me, the union people. I was a porter, so it was the porter reps. Three of them came and pulled me offside and said they had instructions from the trade union headquarters not to supply any services to the new unit. That the management had broken the agreement with the union and I was to have no dealings with the new unit.

The hospital administrator blew a fuse. She said the union people were terrorists, which I fully agreed with. But in fact union headquarters had never said any such thing. It was a lie. It was a minefield. Certain workers ran, they ran that hospital. They behaved as if they were management. It was a case of the tail wagging the dog.

Even doing your legitimate job, it was a cushy number. You never came out of it tired. I work now. I come home and say 'I'm tired', because I'm working now. But over the next five months it started. I listed fourteen incidents of bullying in five months.

And I wasn't the only one. Other porters, they were killed, they were eliminated. Those fellas were cowards. All it takes is one manager to stand up to them, but management wouldn't do it. They gave me a copy of some anti-bullying policy to read . . .

For about nine months it was okay. There was some bullying but I wasn't naïve. I didn't attempt to improve myself financially. They were denying me overtime. They were trying to isolate me. They'd say to me: 'Don't park your car there.' It was so senseless. My wages had shot down.

I was prevented from getting into the hospital. I had to drive round the back. One time I'd had to go out to the post office and I was coming back. There was a woman behind me at the gate and they had to get her to pull back her car, so I could reverse back, away from the entrance. Nine months later I resigned verbally and I told the dole office. That evening I got a call from Jonnie, the union rep, and he said 'We'll get it all fixed. Don't resign, go out sick.' So I went out sick with depression.

I had been threatened and told that I would never get overtime, over my dead body.

I went back to work and I was told there was to be a meeting to discuss my situation. It was at that meeting that I was assaulted by another porter. He just came at me.

I could feel all his power coming through his belly. Then he pushed me back and said he was going to throw me out the window. Several people were there, and they were really shocked.

But nothing happened. I waited months and months and months. The meeting was in November. The hospital manager, the supervisor, Jonnie from the union, your man from personnel. Your man from personnel tried to excuse what had happened.

The big guy, the chief porter, wasn't even questioned until six months later. That was over two men prior to me, who he bullied because he thought that they were homosexual.

In the health service you either keep quiet or speak up and lose your job.

CHRISTOPHER

by Eoin Colfer

ARTICLE 24

Everyone has the right to
rest and leisure, including
reasonable limitation of
working hours and periodic
holidays with pay.

Marco dreamed of lying in fat green grass and gazing at blue sky. Sometimes the dream was so solid in his mind that he thought it must have actually happened. In another life maybe.

A thrown spool of thread knocked his forehead.

'You dreaming about grass again?'

Christopher. Of course. The Kenyan boy's smile was white in his dark face.

'Grass? Grass like fat worms?'

'Caterpillars, stupido,' corrected Marco.

Christopher frowned. 'Cat hair peelers? You are stupido, Marco baby.'

Marco chuckled twice. It took a lot to drag two chuckles out of a person in this place but Christopher could do it.

'You are the stupido, Christopher baby. And you stink like the backside of a sick dog.'

Now Christopher chuckled. 'Backside of a sick dog. This is a prince among insults.'

Heavy footsteps creaked on the floorboards and the boys stopped their joking. Bluto was on the work floor. The factory foreman honked into the phone for a minute then hung up, muttering about whatever new problem the phone call had brought him. This was a dangerous time. Bluto fined people when he was upset.

Marco hunched low into his work, shutting out the universe. This was what Bluto wanted to see in his employees: a good work ethic. On this Sunday Marco was stitching gold wings on the pockets of fake Nike shorts. The wing was the adopted symbol of the AC Milan striker, Costas Andioni.

'Andioni breaks his leg and we're gonna be picking these wings out with our teeth,' Christopher had whispered just loudly enough for everyone to hear, earning himself a clout on the ear and yet another visit to the office.

Mrs M had left the door open so the workers could hear what happened to smart-mouths.

'This ain't no sweatshop, Kenya,' she had shouted, her shrill voice rising to the concrete ceiling. 'You're free to go anytime you want. You want to go, please go. You going, Kenya?'

Christopher shook his head, chin so low it touched his chest.

They have broken him, thought Marco. Even brave, shining Christopher.

But when Christopher returned to his bench, the first thing he did was to ask whether Marco had farted.

Not broken. Still Christopher.

Marco never offered backchat as he could not afford to be docked an hour's pay. Bluto loved to dock wages. Christopher said that whatever Bluto took from you, he kept for himself to buy rare Pokemon cards for his collection. Everyone pulled their weight at Marco's home, even the twins helped to make the foil roses that Mother sold at the city's traffic lights.

'Speedy, Mr Bluto,' Marco would say, hating the man even as he smiled. 'Just the way you like it.'

And so he worked that day. Wing after wing. Gold thread on the inside, red flames feathered around the border. Marco worked without a break until dusk, until his backbone was a glowing rod and his fingers were claws.

Eventually, he leaned back and sighed, his breath pluming like chimney smoke. Mrs M always turned off the heat around midday, claiming that the workers' own industry should keep them warm.

Marco pushed back his chair, tugged at his cushion to make sure it was tied down securely, then walked stiffly towards the bathroom past the thirty or so workers.

In spite of the factory's chill, a dense smell clogged the building.

There was bleach in the mix, and sweat, rubber and oil. Though he knew it was merely a mixture of chemicals, Marco imagined the smell was alive. He could use this in one of his stories.

Marco often wrote stories, most featuring Quantum Boy (Marco himself) and his sidekick, Dreadlock (Christopher of course). Quantum Boy zipped through time getting himself entangled in famous historical adventures and Dreadlock was always on hand with a witty comment at the right time. For example: 'This time you have come up short, Napoleon.'

Marco ducked quickly inside the cramped bathroom. He did not pull the bulb cord, because then Mr Bluto would see the light leaking out under the door and come to hurry him along.

The bathroom was colder than the rest of the building because it wasn't really part of the building. There was a gap one block wide all the way around where the breeze blocks had subsided from the factory proper. The wind whistled through and froze the toilet seat.

And while Marco warmed the seat with his palm, he did not notice the click-clack of Bluto's approaching footsteps. And because there was no light on the floor, Bluto presumed the bathroom was empty.

He barrelled into the cramped space backwards, shouting into his phone. 'I said Tropical Mega Battle, gold edition, you idiot. Not bronze. I won't pay a penny for bronze.'

Bluto did not realise Marco was there until he sat on him. Even then he did not know that it was Marco, because if he had he surely would not have run onto the work floor with his trousers in his hand screaming: 'Toilet monster! It bit me. They are real. I knew it. I knew it.'

The experience was not pleasant for Marco either. One second his life did not seem to be in any immediate danger, and the next there was a sudden overpowering smell of sweat and cheese and his face was mashed by back fat.

Marco stumbled into the factory, squinting and gasping like a prisoner released from his dungeon. 'Sorry,' he coughed, knowing that whatever had happened would be his fault. 'I'm sorry, sir. I must hurry back to work.'

Bluto lurched forward, grabbing Marco's shoulder.

'Tell them, boy. You must have felt it.' Then Bluto stuttered to a halt as the truth became clear. It had been Marco in the bathroom with the lights off. Only Marco.

'No toilet monster,' he breathed, calming himself with gulps of air. 'Just a boy.'

And for a moment he was happy, then the red tint of embarrassment coloured his cheeks. By now every worker in the factory had gathered round – even Mrs M had come from her office to check on the disturbance. She stood, wrapped in her knee-length puffa jacket, glaring at the foreman.

'When I was a child,' explained Bluto. 'My brother told me stories of a monster who lived in the toilet bowl.' It was ridiculous, even to his own ears.

'This boy!' he shouted, hoisting his trousers with one hand. 'Skulking in the bathroom with the light off. He must be docked! Fired!'

Christopher piped up from the throng of workers. 'The toilet monster. He is the one who must be fired.' A few workers tittered but not Bluto. 'Shut your mouth, Kenya. This boy must go.'

'But if Marco goes, who will stitch Andioni's wings?' asked Christopher. 'The toilet monster? His fingers are clumsy and he will drip on the material.'

More laughter now, even Mrs M's mouth was twitching at one corner.

'Please, Mrs M,' pleaded Bluto. 'Fire him now.'

Christopher contorted his face and limbs in a hilarious impression of a dull monster trying to sew.

'Arrrrgh. Dis work be berry difficult for poor toilet monster.'

Bluto dropped Marco and charged at Christopher. The other workers clapped and whooped as Christopher easily dodged the foreman, weaving between the machines. The fun might have lasted for longer, had not Mrs M anticipated Christopher's route and snagged him by the ear as he shot around a corner.

'That's the end of your little game, Kenya,' she snapped. 'Into the office with you.'

Bluto was still in attack mode, but Mrs M froze him with a single pointed finger. 'And you! Prepare my peppermint tea. And in future, whistle before entering the bathroom. Everyone knows that the toilet monster cannot bear whistling.'

'A good joke, Mrs M,' said Christopher, still smiling.

Mrs M shrunk his smile with another tug on the ear, dragging the skinny boy towards her office, where he would surely be fired.

Marco did not know what to do. Quantum Boy would blast Mrs M into the dinosaur age, but Marco had no special powers. He was a scared boy who still hadn't used the bathroom. Though he felt a little guilty, Marco backed into the bathroom, remembering to switch on the light. In the corner of his eye something moved. It was Mrs M. Her office window could be clearly seen through the gap between bathroom and factory wall.

Before Marco realised what he was doing, his arm was through the gap, seeming to pull the rest of him after it.

It was a tight squeeze, but Marco sucked in his ribcage, flattened his nose and managed to inch through the gap until he emerged into the factory yard. The sky was wrong. Where there should be the dark blue of night, there were orange-bellied clouds, reflecting the city's street lights.

Go back, whispered Marco's good sense. *Go back.*

But he did not.

The window blinds were old and missing several slats so Marco's view was barely obstructed. He made a funnel with his hands and looked through it to the room inside.

Mrs M was behind her desk shouting at Christopher, who sat in a wooden chair facing her. She shouted and pounded the desk, making the pens jump.

I must call out to him, thought Marco. Share the blame. Perhaps Mrs M would fine us both and fire neither.

But then Marco noticed that something was not right. Mrs M smiled and even winked at Christopher, who did not seem in the least afraid. As a matter of fact he seemed comfortable and relaxed, propping his knees on the desk and helping himself to some peanuts from a bowl.

Marco moved further along to a spot where the pane was cracked and a dagger-shaped sliver of glass had fallen out.

'Another incident like this and you will be let go, Kenya!' he heard Mrs M say.

'Thank you, Madam,' Christopher said, his white teeth like rows of chewing gum. 'I will be a good worker.'

It was all fake, Marco realised. For the benefit of those listening on the factory floor.

Mrs M spoke again, this time in quiet tones. 'You go too far with Bluto,' she said. 'Your job is to keep the workers happy. Happy workers are hard workers.'

'Bluto was scaring Marco,' said Christopher. 'He is the best one we have.'

Mrs M was impressed by such wisdom. 'You are right, dear Christopher. If Marco had gone, ten more would follow him and the Andioni order would never be finished on time.' She opened her desk drawer and took out a few notes. 'A small bonus for my Trojan horse.'

Christopher took the money and tucked it into his sock. 'You should tell Bluto to leave Marco alone. He is soft but I like him.'

'I will tell him. Now, you go back to work.'

'Five more minutes – a can of Pepsi?'

Mrs M smiled almost tenderly. 'One can. Five minutes, then you go out of here crying like a baby.'

Christopher pushed out his bottom lip.

'No one cries like Christopher,' he said. Then in a typical Christopher motion he popped out of the chair like a circus acrobat and trotted across to a small fridge on the floor. He selected a cola and stretched on the ground to drink it.

'Drink slowly,' Mrs M chided. 'Or you will give yourself a tummy ache.' Christopher's reply was a gentle burp.

Marco turned away from the window. His friend's job was safe, that much was clear. But was his friend his friend?

Dreadlock is gone, he realised. There is only Quantum Boy now.

Marco felt cold and betrayed. Christopher had been masquerading as their comedian, when all the time he was under Mrs M's wing. Even so, I still laughed. Does it matter why he jokes?

It did matter, Marco decided. Christopher's jokes were like glossy red apples with black sludge at their core. He would not laugh again.

Marco felt sick to his stomach and wished that he could just go home. But he knew he must return to the factory. But before he went back inside, Marco allowed himself one last longing look at the lights and life of the city beyond. His mother was out there somewhere, selling foil roses at the traffic lights of east London.

GRACE IN A TREE

by Anne Enright

ARTICLE 25

1. Everyone has the right to a standard of living adequate for the health and wellbeing of themselves and their family, including food, clothing, housing and medical care and necessary social services, and the right to security in the event of unemployment, sickness, disability, widowhood, old age or other lack of livelihood in circumstances beyond their control.

2. Motherhood and childhood are entitled to special care and assistance. All children, whether born in or out of wedlock, shall enjoy the same social protection.

Mary Rose Binchy

I saw Grace in a tree, so I went over to her and said 'Up there for dancing.' She was squatting on one foot with the other leg dangling down and her two arms were spread wide, holding on to the branches. I think it was a sycamore. But she was high enough up there, and she didn't answer the dancing line, despite the fact that the kids used it all the time. Then I had to run back over to one of the kids in question, who was stalled in that place where kids get stuck, just before they start to bawl; there beside the swings in the sunshine. I read somewhere that kids don't cry if there are no adults to see them. I suppose their parents do it the other way around, or try to. We cry when we are alone.

There's me saying, 'It's the onions', weeping at the kitchen counter one day, though for the life of me I could not say what I was weeping for.

And the child who asked me what was wrong, the child I told the lie to, my youngest, he hasn't eaten onions to this day.

Fact.

He is the one who is crying now by the swings. He is crying because I am there to kiss it better. And if I wasn't there, he would just toddle on.

You can't win.

Maybe that was what had Grace up that tree, the never winning thing – where else would you go? I might climb a tree myself on the strength of it. I looked around for her little one – who she called Mary, because when she grew up it would be a really unusual name. But Mary wasn't where I saw her last, trailing that beautiful quiet boy with his microscooter, down the tarmac strip of path.

I hoped she was all right.

These days Mary kept saying that her Daddy was going to pick her up from school, but that was because it wasn't really happening any more. He used to come every now and then, very glamorous and young, making us all feel fat. He drove off with Mary bouncing around in the back of the car, which looked so funny until you realised there was no seatbelt involved. Still he was there. He was at the school gate. Which was to be commended. And we liked the look of him. He didn't even wear a coat; turning up in his T-shirt, he seemed so free.

That was because he was free, I suppose. Unlike us, with another child or two stuck to us as we talked. One day, Cathy Blake told us her husband would be doing the birthday party and all the other weekend stuff, because they had just got a separation, and I had a sudden mad burst of envy.

'Jesus, the whole weekend off,' I said to Grace, who laughed. But you never really knew with Grace, what side she was on in what war. Her situation was never clear. Mary's Dad had come back from England but he didn't live with them, or probably didn't, and you could never tell if Grace wanted him to, or where the money came from, whatever money there was – at a guess it didn't come from him. So sometimes the whole complaining thing, carping about the price of cut flowers or grousing about your husband's smelly socks, seemed like the wrong thing to say.

It made Grace go a bit vague.

'God, the socks,' she might say and give a shrug. But she couldn't do the chit-chat, and sometimes she couldn't do the shrug. And you wondered what went on. She seemed so old. A little slip of a thing and she looked at you sometimes, like what she had to say was so far down a road you would never have to go.

Grace said she came home one day and Mary's father had gone out – something urgent for work – and he had left the child with some guy who was drinking beer on the sofa, some guy she'd never seen before. And he was an okay guy but still.

'But still,' I said.

And we looked at each other, to share the horror.

If she could just let him go, I remember thinking, it might be easier.

If she could just do the whole single thing, or admit to it. I mean, she'd already lived longer than most people – the endless nights she had put in, over the years, alone with that little baby: it's not as if she didn't know the furthest corners of her own young heart.

But then you heard the squeal Mary let out of her when she saw her Daddy in the school yard and you had to leave them to it. Morally that is. You had to let them love each other and muddle through.

Not that he was there, now, most of the time. When you thought about it, it was a good while since he had been around.

So I was watching for Mary, in the playground, as I picked up my little son. I had one eye out, for her amazing hair.

'Will I kiss it? Big kiss? All better.'

I straightened up and had a proper look. Her mother was up a tree and I felt the child should be informed, somehow. I could shout for her, but Mary had something wrong with her ears these days – or maybe that was the problem all along, because there was always something a little delayed about her, a little off the beat; the way she looked at you, as though to wonder what you might do next.

Nothing, you wanted to say to her. I'm not going to do a single thing. She has auburn hair, Mary, real auburn like you might get in a hairdresser's bottle, and thick, creamy skin and eyes that are brown as a monkey's. She's all there – that's the only thing you can say about that child – she is all there.

But the ear thing was a blow, and the landlord was making

noises about selling before the market collapsed. Grace said she couldn't give a shit because Mary was waking at night with the pain and they were both ashen, the two of them, on the morning run.

So the playground – the little bit of good weather, and bumping into pals – was a blessing; the way kids can be happy in an instant, and hare off over the grass, while the mothers stand and let the worry lift off them, like steam in the sunshine.

My own little fella was lifted to rights and trundling off to his next disaster, and my daughter was taking off her clothes and tying them around her waist – coat, sweatshirt, there was no telling where she would stop. And Mary wasn't anywhere that I could see.

It was only when I turned back to Grace that I spotted her. She had appeared under the tree and was looking up at her mother, and she was completely silent – which isn't the word you use about Mary, I don't actually think I had ever seen her standing still. And her mother looked back down at her – she was nuts about that child – and I wondered who would speak first and what they would say.

Because you never know what is going on. No one knew with Cathy Blake either before the separation; herself and Joe the most normal couple you could meet. You never know who cries and who watches them cry, or how people get through.

So Grace sat in her tree, with her arms opened wide and her leg dangling down. And Mary stood looking up at her. The wind went through the leaves and it lifted Mary's hair a little. Then it died down.

'Don't fall, Mammy,' she said.

CHRISTOPHER JENKINS

by Carlo Gébler

ARTICLE 26

1. Everyone has the right to education. Education shall be free, at least in the elementary and fundamental stages. Elementary education shall be compulsory. Technical and professional education shall be made generally available and higher education shall be equally accessible to all on the basis of merit.

2. Education shall be directed to the full development of the human personality and to the strengthening of respect for human rights and fundamental freedoms. It shall promote understanding, tolerance and friendship among all nations, racial or religious groups, and shall further the activities of the United Nations for the maintenance of peace.

3. Parents have the right to choose the kind of education that shall be given to their children.

Brian Maguire

I'm the cleaning orderly and I was buffing the floor when they first brought him onto the wing. This was early December. He'd flat feet, long lank hair, a goatee, buckteeth, a paunch and thick glasses. Kiddy fiddler, I thought. Had to be. You can tell. You're not meant to but you can, believe me. His name was Christopher Jenkins.

He opted for permanent lock-up. Sensible. No aggro. Nobody saw him for weeks. I don't think he even got the Christmas dinner. The screws forgot to bring it to him. Not that anybody cared. He was a root. Why should he be fed?

Then the holidays ended. What a relief. Holidays just meant more time locked in our cells. Early January, normal regime resumed and the first Thursday afternoon of the New Year I slipped into the dining hall. The place was full of prisoners waiting to be called to the workshops or education or visits. He was standing by himself clutching a file of paper and a couple of Biros. Clearly going to education, same as me. Oh no, I thought. In my class? I hoped not. I don't like roots. It's what they've done, obviously. And it's what they attract – idiots who want to make a reputation and clobber them, which sends the prison mad, which brings the peelers in, and then everyone ends up having a bad time.

So as I waited I said, 'Please God, not my creative writing class.' But did He listen? No! When I got into the classroom, he was in the corner.

'Hello, Chalky.' This was Beefy. Armed robber. Doing eight. I sat beside him. He wasn't in my block so I only saw him in class. 'Good Christmas?'

'It's jail.'

'And I thought it was a dream.'

The door opened. The thirteen in the class fell quiet as she came in. Wearing a skirt that swished. And perfume. And earrings that dangled. Our teacher. A woman. With a woman's voice and nice hands. And nail varnish.

'Good break?'

'Yes, Anne,' thirteen men replied eagerly. The class was fine and dandy but really we came for her.

'And who are you?' she said to him in the corner who hadn't spoken.

Christopher Jenkins opened his mouth but the only noise that came out was his tongue slapping inside.

'Ch . . . Chr . . . Chri . . .'

Oh no, I thought, a root with a stammer in my favourite class. 'His name's Christopher Jenkins.'

'Thank you, Chalky.'

'Root lover,' came the quiet words Anne didn't hear. The speaker was Alan, on my left. Drug dealer. Doing six. Unpopular. His measures were always under. Before Christmas some lads, annoyed they never got quite what they paid for, gave him a tanking in the yard. Obviously it hadn't done him any good. He was still as obnoxious as ever. Root lover? Me? *Alan*, I wanted to shout, *I'm doing eight. Actual and grievous bodily harm. On a peeler. When he tried to arrest me, I hit him in the face with a brick. Any more lip out of you and you'll get the same.*

Anne read us a bit of Laurie Lee's *Cider with Rosie*. Then we all had to describe a childhood memory. Then we all read our pieces aloud except Christopher Jenkins. Anne read his. It was about his dad pinning a mouse down with a plastic tube and the mouse running up the inside and jumping into his face. He damned near swallowed it and we all damned near died laughing. Except for Alan that is. He just scowled. Jealous boots, I thought.

Midday, Anne gave us our homework – five hundred words on a parent. Class dismissed.

Back in the block I got my tea from the dining hall. Battered fish. Mushy peas. An ice-lolly. As I walked back along the wing I passed Christopher Jenkins's cell and I couldn't help looking in. He was sitting on his bed picking at his fish.

He saw me looking in and nodded cautiously. I nodded back just as carefully.

'Brilliant story today,' I said.

His tongue started inside his mouth. Finally, after a lot of trouble he said, 'Thank you,' beaming as he spoke. I was probably the first person who'd addressed him nicely since he'd arrived. The next day he borrowed my Sellotape and he returned it the day after with an Aero from the tuck shop. A nodding acquaintance followed. We had the odd game of cards. We walked to education together. Then came a day when I heard myself asking – what was he in for? Naïve and trusting and lonely, he stuttered it out.

He was doing four, he said, for downloading child porn. Did it on the computer at work. Lost his job naturally. Lost his fiancé too. Yeah, I know. How did someone with his looks get a girl? But he did. Or had. Anyhow, she was gone. Ditto family, friends, home. When he got out he'd have to start life from scratch somewhere no one knew him. And he'd be on the register for sex offenders. By the time he'd finished, I felt a bit sorry for him.

In the spring Anne entered everyone's stories in a competition. It was summer when we got the answers. I got a merit and ten quid. Christopher Jenkins came first and won a hundred. Alan, who'd had high hopes for his piece, got nothing, nothing at all. He begged Anne to phone the competition people and check there hadn't been a mistake. He banged on and on about it.

'All right,' said Anne finally. 'I'll go and phone. I'll be five minutes. Don't do anything I wouldn't do.' She walked out. The door closed behind.

'There's a root in the room,' said Alan, suddenly, 'and he's getting on my tits.' The men on either side of Alan nodded.

'If he doesn't go now, he's going to get it.' Here was the deal. Christopher Jenkins either left or else he'd get the traditional punishment because he'd refused an order – not here, it'd be done on the wing: boiling water mixed with sugar in a Nescafé jar, chucked in his face. The boiling sugar, because it would stick to the skin, would ensure the burn went deeper and the scarring was worse than if it was just boiling water on its own.

'There's twenty men back in the block will back me,' continued Alan. 'The root goes.'

'Chris, I'd do what he says,' said Reg. He was a Provo despite his un-Provo name, who'd been brought back after a domestic when he put his wife out the first storey window of their house. 'I'd go.'

I was saying nothing and now Reg, the only other person who talked to him, was telling him this. Christopher Jenkins knew he was out. He gathered his papers and rushed on his flat feet from the room.

'That's better,' said Alan. 'I can breathe easier now.'

The door opened. Anne came in.

'I just saw Christopher at the end of the landing talking to an officer,' she said. 'He said he wasn't feeling well. He wants to be taken back to his block.'

'That's right,' said Alan. 'He's got cancer.' A few laughed. 'Root cancer.' The laughter was louder. Even Reg and Beefy smiled. 'It's fatal I hear. He won't be coming back.'

'Won't he?'

'No, and good thing too,' said Alan.

'I think I'll be the judge of that.'

'We're twelve now, much better than thirteen.'

'I didn't know you were superstitious.'

'You do now,' he said.

When class finished she asked me to stay and as soon as everyone was out she closed the door. She was wearing a silky dress and her hair had a marvellous sheen and we were alone. It should have been the moment of my year, possibly my sentence.

'Who pushed him out?'

'Who?'

'Christopher Jenkins.'

I said nothing. Just looked at her.

'You talk to him. I know it wasn't you. Or Reg. So who did it?'

'This is a prison,' I said.

'That doesn't mean you have to act like it's a prison.'

'Oh yes you do. You know I can't say.'

'No, I don't. Somebody put him out. I want to put him out. You will tell me who.'

'And get a beating, or a scalding.'

The door opened. 'Chalky,' said the officer, 'escort's waiting.'

'I expected better of you,' she said.

'It's jail,' I said, 'don't expect better of anyone in jail. Expect worse.'

'Don't worry,' she said, 'in future I will.' She put me on report – failing to obey an order. I said nothing at the adjudication. The governor gave seven days in the punishment unit. When I got back on the wing I heard Christopher Jenkins had got a scalding anyway. I never went back to Anne's class. Now on Thursday afternoons I'm on gardens. It's good to be in the fresh air.

LEARNING TO GRIEVE FOR OUR ENEMIES

by Hugo Hamilton

ARTICLE 27

1. Everyone has the right freely to participate in the cultural life of the community, to enjoy the arts and to share in scientific advancement and its benefits.

2. Everyone has the right to the protection of the moral and material interests resulting from any scientific, literary or artistic production of which they are the author.

Barrie Cooke

Article 27: Everyone has the right to participate in the cultural life of the community. Sure. Including writing books, making films, sculptures – singing, dancing, playing hurling, drinking, etc.

What else can I think of? Cracking jokes, self-mockery, wearing studs in your eyebrows, hanging around in public parks, spitting, cursing. Even graffiti is an expression of cultural belonging. Isn't it? An alternative culture. Part of what we become as a community, whether we like it or not. Our identity.

So what exactly is that collective cultural life of ours? Is it the sum of what connects us or what separates us? Something that makes us belong and not feel like outsiders? A mark of our unique sense of place? Every movie, every pop song, every book connects us to that free trade of ideas, often rubbing up against each other but ultimately creating that cultural diversity in which we take part, even passively, without having to write a book or paint a picture, or howl out a half-remembered song in the middle of the night on the way home.

We have the freedom to take part in our culture. Provided, of course, we don't exclude other forms of expression in our community. Or feel excluded.

We Irish understand perhaps more than most what it means to be different. We have experienced loss of identity, through history, through a dying language, through emigration and poverty, through our ultimate expression of freedom and self-determination. It is the dispossessed who need identity most, something which is replaced through songs and stories, through imaginary forms. We have become good at doing that now. We have placed ourselves on the world stage. In fact, our identity has now become a global trade mark, a commodity in many ways.

Our appeal comes from our difference, our island ways, our

faith and nationhood, our light-heartedness, our ability to do business and still make it look like fun. Proud to celebrate the structures of separation, we see ourselves often as either Catholic or Protestant, British or Irish, man or woman, fish or fowl. It has been difficult to be in between. But now those boundaries have become blurred and it's possible to take on multiple forms of belonging without feeling like an outsider.

The Northern peace process is perhaps the most glittering example of this sharing of identity, the ability to step outside the electric fence which is often erected to protect each form of culture and expression. Conflict has made us different.

Peace makes us share that difference.

Nowhere have I experienced this convergence of divisions more recently than at the memorial set up in Ypres to the Irish people who fell in Flanders during the First World War. This war which played such a major role in the Irish way of dealing with the past has been explored by writers like Frank McGuinness and Sebastian Barry, tracking the great difficulties of coming to terms with this episode, including our inability to grieve for those who were wrong-footed by the glorious history of our own independence.

Outside Ypres, the Irish government has since erected a monument in the shape of a round tower, commemorating those who died on the wrong side, so to speak. It is a moving place to visit. For me in particular, because I had a grandfather who died during that war on the British side and was subsequently denied by his own son because he didn't fit into the new Ireland.

A vivid memory from my boyhood is that of wearing the poppy only once in my life, bought for me on Armistice Day by a Protestant neighbour on our street, and ripped from my Aran sweater only a few minutes later as I proudly walked in the door and then thrown into the fire. We grew up being careful who to be sad for.

Last year, I travelled to Ypres with the Irish novelist Dermot Bolger, who has also written extensively about this war and about the life of the Irish poet Francis Ledwidge, who met his death in the fighting there. We were taken on a tour by the director of the Ypres museum, Piet Schielens, who showed us the trenches and pointed to fields where they are still digging up bodies almost a century later. We saw the many graves, lines of white headstones, mostly belonging to boys, young men under twenty-three.

The sky was low. The mist hung in the fields, creating a calmness that felt more like a temporary lull in the fighting. We were told that not infrequently, a grenade explodes on a farm in these parts, killing yet another innocent person so many years later. And each year brings new discoveries, such as the handwritten entry in a cemetery log book in which a family from Tipperary wrote: 'So glad we found you here at last, grandfather. *Go ndéana Dia trocaire air do anam.*'

The Belfast poet Michael Longley writes with great subtlety about his own father's part in the First World War, describing how he received a medal for bravery when he led his unit out to kill a detachment of German soldiers who had strayed into their sights, including the chilling notion of 'mopping up' those Germans still left alive after the battle.

Other writers seem unable, however, to see that conflict with any such clarity, only as a great British tragedy.

British identity still requires the heroic status of victory in order to justify its own history and sense of place in the world. German grief and German limbs in trees become rubbed out by the constant reiteration of German culpability. Chemical warfare simplified by the schoolyard logic that they started it, that they were the ones who invented gas attacks first.

The lull in the fighting doesn't last long in Flanders. It feels at times as though the young soldiers underground have been conscripted to fight forever, again and again, each year, for honour, for valour, 'for empire'.

It is a sad place. Buses full of relatives and tourists come each year in large numbers to grieve for those who fell for their country. At six o'clock every evening, they gather under the great arch in the town where the last post is played and where poppies are laid for the dead, for the missing, for those who were never identified and have no graves.

And afterwards the British visitors wander around the town, reconstructed beautifully in spite of Churchill's wish to maintain it as a ruin. They are seen in the many pubs and restaurants; they buy souvenirs, helmets, bits of shrapnel, cartridges, bits of war memorabilia that will continue to keep the memory of this conflict with them after they go home.

In contrast, the Germans come quietly, in families. They visit the German cemetery, where, famously, a battalion of young German cadets was ordered to march straight to their death into a volley of enemy gunfire in order to demonstrate their loyalty and their courage. The Germans leave quietly afterwards. They are not seen in the town. They don't buy souvenirs and they don't talk about bravery.

Bravery, this key word which Michael Longley got from his father's citation, is not prized in German cultural expression. Because bravery – *Mut* or *Tapferkeit* – is not such a heroic concept any more, but something generic which is required for any act in the face of danger, something prized as much by the SS, a slippery virtue that can be attributed also to a freedom fighter, a hunger striker, a terrorist on either side of a conflict.

Grieving is part of our cultural life. Remembering the past and the people who died is an important element of our identity. But how much more difficult and creative and culturally imaginative is it to be able to grieve for the fallen enemy also? How much further along the road to reconciliation have we travelled when we step into the shoes of the other?

It seems as though the war in Flanders is sometimes destined to remain in the trenches. That reconciliation which I have personally had to make between my Irish grandfather and my German grandfather, both combatants in that war, both casualties, still seems hard to achieve in Flanders.

I asked myself if it would ever be possible for the British to commemorate their dead alongside the German dead in one single act of remembrance. There are poppies seen in Ypres with Irish tricolour backing. It's hard to imagine poppies combined with German flags, but who knows, it might be the kind of collective cultural European expression of grief that would give those underground the repose they deserve, to think that those above ground have come to terms with history.

AN ANTHEM FOR THE KING

by Kevin Barry

ARTICLE 28

Everyone is entitled to a
social and international
order in which the rights and
freedoms set forth in this
Declaration can be fully realised.

Alan Clarke

At this moment, under grandma's skirts, Wee Frankie had a crayon clamped in his wee
left mitt and was scrawling free verse on the floor.

Then the old king died, and the TV played sombre martial music, and we all wailed and beat our fists off the walls, and we ate buttery, potato-based dishes for comfort. But then the king-to-be was named, and he seemed pretty laidback and easy-going, so everybody on the island was cool with the situation.

There was massive excitement above in the shack, of course – the king-to-be was due to call around. We were the island's foremost family of musicians, and as was the custom, a new king meant a new anthem, and we had always written the island's anthems. An ear for a tune and a way with sentimental words: that old stuff is in the blood.

It was a crazy scene. Grandma swept the dirt floor with her hardwire brush and she almost hovered she was back and forth across that floor so fast, her full skirts twirling as she went. Cousin Ely restrung his banjo and gave the drum machine an overhaul. The twins, Dodo and Bess, hung from the rafters small coloured lights they'd fashioned from hand-caught fireflies. Uncle Joe roused himself from his maudlin nature to practise hot licks on the electric geetar. Sis, our ace wordsmith, made notes for the new anthem's lyrics, while Grandpa rinsed his throat with raw alcohol to prepare those mighty vocal cords. I tried out some weird new dance moves and Wee Frankie yodelled his in-fill harmonies. We had all washed our hair and put on fresh-pressed dungarees.

'Now I'm just thinkin' out loud here,' said Sis, looking up from her notes. 'See what y'all reckon . . .'

We gathered in.

'Way I'm thinkin',' she said, 'we open with a fairly vague verse about general principles. About how we like things on the island to be mellow and relaxed, with lots of impromptu hugs and unguarded laughter.'

'Absolutely,' said Grandpa. 'We keep it fluffy.'

'Then we go into a feel-good chorus, with more of the peace-and-love hoopla, and then we slide in a second verse that has a go at the crowd over.'

'Over' meant the closest of our neighbour islands in the archipelago.

'About how they tried to pass off their filthy slattern morals on us?' suggested Uncle Joe.

'Ad lib to fade,' said Sis. 'Now we'll need a tune that's instantly memorable and capable of being whistled by even the magnificently deranged.'

'I'm on it,' said Grandpa, and he started rifling through his Carpenters songbook.

Bugles sounded, then the clatter of donkey hooves: the king-to-be had arrived. Announced by drooling flunkies, he was soon among us, and we instantly liked the cut of his jib. He was wry, open-faced and jaunty, with a featherweight's spring in his nimble step, and also he was charmingly myopic, he kept walking into the walls of the shack and tripping over our little sugán chairs. The greetings eventually done with (these took several hours) he sprawled out humbly on the dirt floor and listened to our ideas for the new anthem. Uncle Joe essayed some Valiumy, Carpenters-type riffs on the geetar, while Sis warbled a bunch of fresh lyrics about hand-holding, meadows full of buttercups, and knock-kneed little fauns.

'I'm lovin' it,' said the king-to-be. 'Kind of an easy-listenin' feel?'

'Fluffy,' said Grandpa.

'I'm totally down with fluffy,' said the king-to-be.

Then Sis improvised a verse about the crowd over, about how they were sly and intemperate and unusually prone to venereal diseases.

'Time-out!' cried the king-to-be. 'Jesus, people, I'm tryin' to open up a diplomatic channel there! We're gonna have to lay off the crowd over.'

'So we go with fluffy all the way through?' said Grandma.

'Not at all,' said the king-to-be. 'Actually, I think we could use the anthem to lay down some new ground rules for the island.'

'Oh?'

'For example,' he said, 'it'd be nice to let the gingers know where they can go sling it.'

With a deft scoop of her arm, Grandma swept up Wee Frankie, who was ginger as the day was long, and concealed him beneath her full skirts. Our short-sighted new royal luckily hadn't made Frankie for a carrot-top.

'Oh I don't like them redheads one bit!' snarled the king-to-be. 'They have dreadful complexions and they can't take a tan! They take the look off the place something rotten. Gingers will ne'er again walk the villages of this island so long as I'm suckin' air! We can work this in, yes?'

'See what I can do,' mumbled Sis.

'Also, citogs,' said the king-to-be.

'Huh?'

'Citogs!' he cried. 'Left-handed folks! I hate them big! The citogs are going to be rounded up and driven to the swamp with the gingers.'

We shuddered. The swamp of the island was a bad-mood swamp, bleak and desolate, and prone to easterly winds, big rats, and dark magic. It was where we kept the gypsies.

'Citogs,' said the king-to-be, 'are unpleasantly arty and bohemian. They always strike me as a bit superior.'

At this moment, under Grandma's skirts, Wee Frankie had a crayon clamped in his wee left mitt and he was scrawling free verse on the floor. Poems about love and consciousness. In Latin.

'And while we're at it,' said the king-to-be, 'there's the letter R. People who can't say their Rs make my skin crawl! Anyone who calls a rabbit a wabbit? They're going to the swamp!'

Small consolation here, for Wee Frankie, thanks be to Jesus, had no problem with his Rs.

The king-to-be departed then – he had an appointment to try out some new robes and harlots – and he left us to compose the hateful new anthem. It was to be debuted at the coronation ceremony next day. The shack fell into a sulk. We paced the dirt floor. Night fell. We moved out to the porch, as was our moon-gazing habit, and we chewed disconsolately on our corncob pipes. Grandpa stared out to the immensity of the night – it's Big Sky up here in the hill country of the interior, the sky was hung with strings of stars, and clouds passed over the moon, like moods across a fat man's face. Grandpa gazed with great sorrow then at Wee Frankie, who was squatting on the floor of the porch, skulling rough wine straight from the bottle and working on a libretto for an opera of his own composing. About astrophysics.

'We can't do it,' said Grandpa.

'Ah we haven't a choice,' said Grandma. 'We do the anthem. Then we dye Frankie's hair and we bate him right-handed!'

'No,' said Grandpa. 'I just won't be a party to it.'

But we were against the tide. All over the archipelago, it had become fashionable to deride gingers. Citogs, too, had taken a bad press. And people who had trouble with their Rs were routinely made fun of on the cable talk shows.

'Lookit,' said Grandma. 'We'd all like to live in an archipelago where gingers, citogs and people who can't say their Rs live freely and openly. It's a very pretty idea. But that archipelago is a fantasy, Gramps! It don't exist.'

'Then we make it exist,' said Grandpa, huskily, and we all teared up some.

'But how?' cried Grandma.

'One island at a time,' said Grandpa, and there wasn't a dry eye on the porch.

It was at this point Wee Frankie hopped up on the porch rail and expressed himself through the language of dance.

The morning of the coronation dawned hot and misty. From everywhere on the island (except the swamp) the people thronged down to the Great Glen: they were shitfaced on moonshine and patriotism. We took to the stage just before noon. We launched into some slow-building power chords and percussion riffs to get the vast crowd a-swayin' and a-hollerin'. We let it build and build and build until the crowd was ready to be wrung out like a dishcloth. Okay, so it was a direct lift from the intro to 'Gloria' on Van Morrison's *Them*, but who was gonna sue? The new king was up out of his throne, jiggin' like a fool, eating chicken wings, and snogging harlots. I did some of the weird dance moves and the crowd went loolah altogether. Then Grandma put down her bodhrán and took centre stage. She raised her hands to hush the crowd, and she leaned back, and Dodo and Bess went all spooky and rattly with the tambourines – kssss-kssss-kssss! kssss-kssss-kssss! – and then Grandma lifted high her full skirts, and everybody gasped: out strode Wee Frankie.

With his ginger locks glistening in the noonday sun, Wee Frankie swaggered forward, and though he was only three years of age and three foot tall, he had the walk and carry of a pure man. He went to the front of the stage, and he grabbed the mic in his wee left mitt, and he looked up to the throne, and he eyeballed the new king, and he cried out:

'Awight! Awe we weady to wock'n'woll?'

A great roar built, and a strange, powerful surge moved through the crowd, it rippled and throbbed like a python loosed, and there was no way it could be held back or arrested – it had the feel of a muscle flexing.

FREE AND FULL

by Glenn Patterson

ARTICLE 29

1. Everyone has duties to the community in which alone the free and full development of his personality is possible.

2. In the exercise of his rights and freedoms, everyone shall be subject only to such limitations as are determined by law solely for the purpose of securing due recognition and respect for the rights and freedoms of others and of meeting the just requirements of morality, public order and the general welfare in a democratic society.

3. These rights and freedoms may in no case be exercised contrary to the purposes and principles of the United Nations.

Weeks he had been looking at it. Every day, five times a day. Once or twice, waking in the early hours, he had risked the landing, past the children's bedroom doors, and switched on the lamp above his desk to look at it some more. To tell you the truth he was sorry now he had ever picked it. He said to his wife, you know the way when you were a kid and you were at a party and there was a plate of buns and you got first dibs? You know the way you'd be torn between going for the one you really wanted and the thought that there were still ten other kids to choose after you? And they were watching you, the grownup with the plate was watching you, and you panicked and closed your fingers around something, anything, and the plate passed on and you looked down at your hand and thought: *Oh, great. Bakewell pissing tart. That's what I've done. I've picked the Bakewell tart of the convention.*

Not that he would ever have let on to anyone but her. And then, too, he must have had something in mind when he sent the email: 'I'll do 29.' What he had in mind in all likelihood was the attitude, common in Northern Ireland, that rights were a zero-sum game, that the granting of them to one community (a word, incidentally, which he despised) resulted in a loss of them for another, the other. Like the confrontations over Orange parades. He had once proposed that the residents of the areas the parades wanted to pass through respect the Order's right to march, while the Order respected the residents' right not to be disturbed or offended. He foresaw a standoff while it was determined whose protection of the other's rights should prevail, but in the end, he suggested, it ought to be settled without bloodshed.

He had thought about revisiting this idea as fiction. 'The Bridge' (he had Ormeau in mind, but he would abstract it from that, abstract it, if he was able, out of Northern Ireland altogether): offenders at one end, offended at the other, only halfway through the story would flip and the offenders would become the offended and vice versa. The epigraph would be a line from 'After the Fire' by John Hewitt: 'You must give freedom if you would be free.' But he wondered if there wasn't something a little dishonest at the heart of this; whether the moment for such a story, however abstracted, had gone.

He looked at the article (Tarticle) again. Five times that day, five days the next. This had all got a bit ridiculous.

It had got so ridiculous he was taking refuge in the third person.

It had got so ridiculous he was packing up to leave the country.

India. Festival. Whatever the problem, there was always a festival where you could lie low for a couple of days.

The hotel was a short distance from New Delhi airport across the road from the building site for a massive shopping mall. (He watched, as he passed, the workmen clamber up their Keystone Kop ladders, imagined the sign at the site entrance: 'No hat? No boots? No problem!') Shanties of the most basic kind bordered the road in-between: polythene and cardboard held together with string and populated at that time of the day almost entirely by dogs and children.

He had been briefed to expect, and if at all possible ignore, the importuning of street kids. If he gave to one he would be approached by another and another and another and even if he gave to all of them, emptied his pockets completely, there would be still others just as needy – needier – trailing after him. No, if he really wanted to help he should wait until he was home, pick a charity with the necessary experience and expertise and set up a direct debit. Not as sexy perhaps as an open wallet, but a darned sight more effective.

The first hotel room he was shown to had a walk-in shower, but no bath. He phoned the desk and asked to be moved: his back. He had told the organisers, he didn't mind where they put him so long as there was a bath. He soaked until the water turned cold then slept as well as could be expected given the flight, the five and a half hour bounce forward in time, and the noise of the air conditioning, even on its lowest, just-about-breathable setting. Next day he passed up the offer of a sightseeing tour to practise his reading: the reason he had been asked here after all. The pool had been emptied for cleaning, but the sun-loungers were out and on colder days than this at home people took to the beaches in their droves. He locked his hands behind his head, book facedown on his chest. Gardeners roamed the grounds in pairs conversing like seminarians, dropping to their knees now and then to pluck out a weed, tend to a border. Over the boundary wall the arms of the building site cranes moved almost imperceptibly until they had told off the entire working day.

Darkness fell while he was waiting in the lobby for the car to take him to the venue. Fell was the word. One minute it was light, the next minute it wasn't. He was struck, on the journey, by how completely the roadside shanties had vanished: no electricity, of course, to announce their presence, no power of any description.

At one set of traffic lights a beggar thumped the windscreen with the stump of his amputated arm. It might have been a fly for all the notice the driver took. At the next set of lights, as though to confirm the logic of the briefing, there was a double thump: a double amputee. The driver checked a text on his mobile phone.

The reading, in a compound on the edge of the embassy

district, was over in less than an hour. Someone asked him during the QA what he was working on and he mentioned 'The Bridge' and it got a laugh and he began to think that there might be something in it after all. At the drinks reception that followed he was offered Guinness and fish tikka. 'More Irish than oysters,' he said, before popping the fish into his mouth. He talked to a man whose best friend was a consultant at a hospital in Belfast; agreed with him it was a small, small world. He left the Guinness alone after the first glass and moved on to white wine. (More Irish these days than stout.) He left the food alone altogether, kept drinking.

On the journey back to the hotel he nodded off. He woke to a tapping on the glass by his ear. A child – girl or boy, he couldn't tell because of the plastic shower cap pulled down low on the forehead – stood by the window, chin level with the chrome rim, holding in its left hand a stick to which were attached the most half-hearted balloons he had ever seen. With the other hand the child motioned to its mouth: eat.

Instinctively he reached for his wallet, ignoring the driver who was speaking to him in English, shouting at the child in Hindi. He got the window down and pressed a note into the child's hand just as the lights changed. He and the child looked at it at the same time: ten rupees. They looked at the notes sticking out of the wallet, the twenties and fifties. They looked at each other. The driver put the car in gear and stepped on the accelerator.

Back in the hotel he sat at the bar doing sums in his notebook. The answers kept coming out the same: about twelve and a half p, ten rupees. He charged the drinks to his room rather than have to face for the moment how much his three gins came to. He didn't bother with a bath.

He woke in the night and thought about calling a taxi, retracing his route, see could he find the child. (The shower cap ought to help. What was that, anyway? Protection? Decoration?) Make up the ten rupees at the very least to whatever he'd spent in the bar. And as he lay there arguing the toss with himself he picked up the notebook again from the bedside table and started to write: the landing at home, the buns, the briefing, the reading, the child in the shower cap with the limp balloons; the expression on its face as it looked from the money in its hand to the notes that never left the wallet.

Day was already breaking by the time he set the notebook down and lay back satisfied that he had at least done something, discharged his writer's duty.

But when he read over what he had written two mornings later on the taxi ride to the airport he didn't think he had done enough at all. Not nearly enough.

And neither do I.

DOMESTIC DECLARATIONS

by Gerard Stembridge

ARTICLE 30

Nothing in this Declaration
may be interpreted as
implying for any State,
group or person any
right to engage in any
activity or to perform
any act aimed at
the destruction of any
of the rights and freedoms
set forth herein.

The twins were excited. It was nearly a year since Mum and Dad last had a night out and left them with the babysitter. Now that they were so much more grown-up, they wondered how much freedom would be allowed. By coincidence in school earlier that day their teacher had been telling their class about the Universal Declaration of Human Rights. Younger twin particularly had been very impressed. Here was the perfect chance to put the theory to the test.

'Dad, have we got human rights?'

'Of course you have.'

'While you're out tonight, have we the right to eat whatever we want from the fridge.'

'Or the freezer.'

'Or the freezer.'

'Yes. You have the right.'

'Can we stay up until ten o'clock?'

'No.'

'Half nine?'

'Yes.'

This was going well. They had been chancing their arm with ten o'clock anyway.

'And before we go to bed have we the right to watch whatever we like on TV?'

'Yes.'

'Or use PlayStation?'

'Yes.'

'Or phone our friends?'

'Yes.'

This was very important. The twins had to use the landline because they were still considered too young to have mobile phones, even though that was a silly idea, and several of their friends had them already.

'However . . .'

The twins looked at each other. Here we go with Dad's 'howevers'. If you get something you have to give something.

'You can eat anything you want, but you can't take all of anything. Don't eat all the cake. Don't drink all the milk. Leave some for the rest of us. It's our right too.'

The twins nodded. Fair enough. Mum was next.

'You can stay up until nine-thirty, but you get into your pyjamas at nine and no acting up with Linda.'

But it was fun to try and get the babysitter to let them stay later. The twins saw the look in Mum's eye, sighed and agreed, even though Elder thought that his sister, being three minutes younger and a girl, should have to go to bed first. Dad was still going on with his 'howevers'.

' . . . so you have to agree on what to watch, and watch quietly. Don't annoy Linda.'

That was easy. Linda was nice, she never got annoyed. She just lounged on the sofa texting her friends and talking to her boyfriend.

' . . . and of course you can use the phone as long as it doesn't prevent Mum or me from ringing home to check that everything's all right.'

The twins nodded automatically. A few seconds passed before something dawned on Younger.

'But . . . but . . . if we're talking on the phone, it will be engaged, so that means you can't call.'

'Good point.'

'But . . . would that mean that we can't use the phone at all?'

'Actually, yes. That's right.'

Elder only got it now.

'Hey! That's not fair.'

'You said we could call our friends.'

'Yes absolutely, you have the right to call your friends, but if you do, then we can't call you, do you understand?'

Mum joined in gently.

'It's a question of which is more important, darlings.'

'Mum always worries about your safety and security when we're out at night. You know we always ring to check that everything's OK. If the phone is engaged we can't do that.'

'It's for your protection. Don't worry.'

The twins were outraged. Both of them had promised their friends that they would ring them tonight.

'But you said we had the right . . .'

'It's not a big deal if you can't phone your pals tonight.'

Elder tried some negotiation.

'Okay. What if we can make one call each. Five minutes each. Then the rest of the time will be free for you to call.'

Dad shook his head. He had that really determined look.

'No you see we don't know when we'll get a chance to call, and if the phone is engaged, we won't know if it's you calling your friends or something much more frightening. Has someone broken into the house and cut off the phone? Are you in terrible danger?'

'You could ring Linda's phone.' Elder was pleading now.

'No, we have no right to ask Linda not to use her private phone just in case we want to ring her.'

The twins were getting desperate. Younger thought of a solution.

'What if our friends ring us?'

'I'm glad you mentioned that. Only Linda is allowed to answer the phone and we'll tell her to get whoever it is off the line as quickly as possible.'

'Unless it's us,' smiled Mum.

'Naturally, unless it's us,' Dad laughed.

Mum could see how upset the twins were. Especially Younger, who tended to be more sensitive about things. She spoke gently to her daughter.

'Darling, I know it seems on the surface to be a sort of contradiction in terms . . .'

Younger wondered was 'contradiction in terms' a fancy adult way of saying 'we're taking your rights away'.

' . . . but in the long run you'll see that what we're doing is for the best. There are so many dangers out there, and I'd feel terrible if anything happened to you and it was our fault for not taking enough care. So trust us on this, okay?'

Further discussion was clearly pointless. The parents left as soon as Linda arrived. She made herself some coffee and curled up on the sofa. The twins put on a DVD, but the sound of Linda's laughter as she chatted freely on her mobile was particularly annoying in the circumstances. Elder got himself some ice cream and seemed happy enough, but Younger just couldn't get the unfairness of it all out of her head. She was angry with her Dad especially. It felt like he was making a fool of her. How could she trust him in future? She couldn't stop brooding on it. Out of her anger and frustration came an idea. Pretending to go to the bathroom, she left Elder and Linda in the living room. Alone in the hall she stared at the telephone she had the right to use but was not allowed to use. She made up her mind, eased down on her hands and knees and crawled under the little table. Very quietly and carefully she took hold of the plug for the phone and eased it out oh-so-slightly, until she broke the connection. The little light on the base went out. The phone still looked plugged in, but no one could now call home.

Younger rejoined the others in the living room. When Mum or Dad phoned to check they wouldn't be able to get through. They would ring again and again. There would be panic. Linda's phone would be engaged. They might even come rushing home and their night out would be ruined. Even when they discovered the problem with the plug there was no way to prove that it was deliberate. Dad might suspect, but he couldn't catch her out. Younger smiled a secret smile.

She could be a right little terror that one. When she didn't get her rights.

CUSTOMERS ALSO BOUGHT . . .

by Ross O'Carroll-Kelly

ARTICLE 31

1. Everyone has the right to do the wrong thing for the right reasons and the right thing for the wrong reasons.

2. Everyone has duties to the community. Sometimes the biggest crime against humanity is to stand by and do nothing at all.

For as long as I've known her, Sorcha's always been heavily into, like, world affairs and shit. As in, that Amnesty newsletter would drop through the letterbox and no sooner did she have it read than she was off, chaining herself to the railings of some embassy or other.

Or storving herself.

Those forty-eight hour Christmas fasts in support of Aung San Suu Kyi had the double effect of highlighting the plight of her favourite prisoner of conscience and allowing her to squeeze into some, I don't know, Marchesa creation for the Berkeley Court New Year ball.

But the only time I was ever, like, actually worried about her was the time they bombed, I don't know, Iran or Iraq or whichever one it was.

Sorcha had been banging on about Saddam Hussein for years – what he'd done to this shower, what he'd done to that shower. At school, she had, like, hundreds of postcords – bodies all over the shop – and she used to send them to, like, TDs and all sorts, demanding that the world do something about this dude.

I could never work out, roysh, why, when they finally did decide to off him, Sorcha suddenly switched sides. But I do remember her telling me one day that she was going on that big morch in town, as in Stop the War, blahdy blahdy blah.

When I mentioned the postcords, she gave me this total filthy and went, 'They're not doing it for humanitarian reasons, Ross.

'They're going to kill, like, hundreds of thousands of innocent people and it's all about oil!' I remember, like, watching the morch on TV – I was actually flicking between it and whatever Grand Prix was on – and actually seeing Sorcha, pretty near the front, standing next to this obvious tosspot.

Goatee, stupid glasses – like that focking John Lennon used to wear.

Never saw him before in my life, roysh, but over the next couple of years I'd hear quite a bit about him. His name was Quicky Fingers. Or maybe Quick E-Fingers – I never visited his ridiculous blog. But Sorcha did, regularly, and she fell under his – I suppose you'd have to say – spell.

Honestly, for the next, like, two years, she barely said a sentence that didn't stort with the words, 'Quicky Fingers says . . . ' It was, 'Quicky Fingers says America only became interested in East Timor when it was in, like, their strategic interest to be.' Or it was, 'Quicky Fingers says that, far from working together, Saddam Hussein and Al Qaeda actually hate each other.' She actually changed as well? As in her personality? She was suddenly, like, picking rows with me, especially after she'd been on the Wolfe to him or maybe met him for, like, coffee. She'd tell me I was, like, unaware of what was happening in the world and she'd say it like it was an actual bad thing.

See, my attitude has always been, what's the point in, like, learning loads of shit when it's all there on the internet if you ever need it.

I'm pretty sure Quicky was trying to get his famous Fingers into her Alan Whickers as well. Anyway, let's just say it was a big build-up of things, but I wanted to deck the goy for a long, long time. The dude had it coming – and in a major way.

The problem was, you can't just walk up to someone and deck them. You have to have, like, a reason? Anyway, I got it one Saturday morning. I was in the sack, watching one of Sorcha's Davina McCall exercise DVDs when my phone rings and it's, like, Aoife – as in her friend? She's in, like, tears. Says she's really worried about Sorcha. Turns out Quicky and a couple of his mates were bringing her to Shannon – Limerick, which was dangerous enough by itself – to do damage to some American navy plane or other. According to Aoife, Quicky had given her a wire-cutters and a hammer.

They were in the Amnesty Freedom Café when I walked in, drinking their Fairtrade whatevers. There was, like, six or seven of them, including Sorcha, sitting in a circle around Quicky, who was obviously loving the attention.

He's like, 'See, that's what the military industrial complex want you to believe. What America really wants is, like, one giant global superstate, which'll be controlled by corporations. Look at the way they already control the UN, the World Bank, the International Monetary Fund, the World Trade Organisation. Why do you think they've been involved in, like, 133 wars and military interventions over the past hundred years? Seriously, man – there's a full list of them on my blog.

'It's, like, don't tell me that Saddam Hussein's a monster – er, you supported him? Like you did Pinochet, Suharto, Duvalier and anyone else you care to mention. Again, there's a full list on the blog.

'And they say it's about human rights, democracy and civil liberties! Er, right. Customers who bought this item also bought Saddam Hussein Is Building A Nuclear Bomb To Drop On Israel and America Didn't Blow Up The Twin Towers Themselves?'

They're all so in awe of him, roysh, that it's a good five minutes before Sorcha even notices I've arrived and even then, it's like she's embarrassed to see me? She introduces me to the whole crew. Firestarter. Fantam 8. They all have, like, e-mail aliases instead of actual names.

Quicky looks at me, then at the logo on my t-shirt – had the old pink Apple Crumble on – smiles and shakes his head, as in, like, pityingly? I'm there, 'Have you got a problem, dude?' but he holds his hands up, still grinning, as if to say, I could say something but I'm not going to.

Someone in the group had given Sorcha a book. *Manufacturing Consent*. I pick it up, flick through it. I focking hate small writing.

Fantam 8 says what he'd love to do one day is just, like, take off somewhere where there's, like, no distractions, for two weeks, and read everything that Noam Chomsky has, like, ever written. And one of the girls – the original bucket of ormpits – says Chomsky is, like, oh my God, so cool and so right about, like, everything.

This obviously stirs something in Quicky because he's off again. 'I mean, yeah, America just makes me want to puke.

'Like, really puke. How dare they tell us that they want to bring freedom and dignity to the people of the world. Check out my blog – this is the country that refused to adopt the Kyoto Protocol, despite being by far the world's biggest polluter?

'Check out what I also have to say about the melting point of the steel contained in the Twin Towers.

'These people care about people's rights? Er, customers who bought this item also bought America And Their NATO Cronies Bombed Yugoslavia Because They Actually Cared About The Suffering Of The Muslims There and George W. Bush Didn't Steal The Presidency From Al Gore?'

I actually can't listen to any more of this shit, even though I haven't a bog what he's on about. I'm looking at Sorcha, roysh, nodding away and I'm thinking, this isn't her. These aren't her kind of people.

'Did you give my wife a hammer and a wire-cutters?' I suddenly go.

Sorcha looks at me, her mouth open. Quicky doesn't look at

me. He looks at the others, sort of, like, rolling his eyes and shaking his head.

I'm there, 'Hey – I'm talking to you.' Quicky looks at my T-shirt again and goes, 'Look, Jock Boy, you've obviously got some kind of American thing going on here . . .'

I'm like, 'Yeah? Well, put this on your blog. I want you outside. As in, outside the Freedom Café? As in, now?'

Sorcha puts her hands up to her boat race and goes, 'Ross, no! You know how much I hate violence.'

Quicky stands up and goes, 'After you.'

NOTES ON THE CONTRIBUTORS

Robert Ballagh was born, and lives, in Dublin. A painter and designer, his work has been exhibited all around the world, and his paintings are held in collections in a number of museums and galleries.

Kevin Barry's first collection of short stories, *There Are Little Kingdoms*, won the Rooney Prize for Irish Literature in 2007. His stage adaptation of the book will be produced in Washington, DC, in 2010. His screenplay, *Memorabila*, is in development with the Irish Film Board. He lives in County Sligo.

Maeve Binchy was born, and lives, in Dublin. Author of many international best-selling novels and short-story collections, her books have been translated into over forty languages, and several have been adapted for stage, film and television.

Mary Rose Binchy is a First Class Honours Graduate of the National College of Art and Design, Dublin. She works as a painter and printmaker and exhibits regularly throughout Ireland and overseas. She lives and works in Dublin.

Dermot Bolger was born, and lives, in Dublin. He has published nine novels, eight volumes of poetry and over twenty plays, and has edited many anthologies. He has received numerous literary awards and is co-founder and executive editor of New Island Books.

John Boyne is the author of seven novels, including the international best-sellers *The Boy in the Striped Pyjamas*, which was made into a Miramax feature film, and *The House of Special Purpose*. The winner of two Irish Book Awards, his novels are published in over forty languages. He lives in Dublin.

Alan Clarke is a painter, illustrator and designer. He has completed numerous commissions in Ireland and abroad, including children's books, murals, conceptual design work for animation and TV, book covers and political caricatures. He has exhibited in Ireland, Europe, the USA and Japan. He lives in Dublin.

Eoin Colfer was born, and lives, in Wexford town. He is the author of several international best-selling novels, including the Artemis Fowl series, *The Wish List*, *The Supernaturalist* and, most recently, the sixth instalment of *The Hitchhiker's Guide to the Galaxy*.

John Connolly was born in Dublin in 1968 and is the author of twelve books, including *The Book of Lost Things*, the Charlie Parker series of mystery novels, and his latest novel, *The Gates*. He divides his time between Dublin and Portland, Maine.

Barrie Cooke was born in Cheshire and has been based in Ireland since 1954. Renowned for his expressionist semi-abstract paintings, he has exhibited widely throughout Europe, the US and Canada. He lives in County Sligo.

Roddy Doyle was born, and lives, in Dublin. A novelist, dramatist and scriptwriter, his novels include *Paddy Clarke Ha Ha Ha*, which won the 1993 Man Booker Prize.

Anne Enright was born in Dublin. She has published essays, short stories, a nonfiction book and four novels. Her novel *The Gathering* won the 2007 Man Booker Prize. She lives in County Wicklow.

Zlata Filipović was born in Sarajevo. Author of *Zlata's Diary: A Child's Life in Wartime Sarajevo* and editor of *Stolen Voices*, a book about young people's war diaries. She holds a BA from Oxford University and an MPhil from Trinity College Dublin. She serves on the board of Amnesty International (Ireland) and has worked with organisations such as the Anne Frank House, UNESCO and UNICEF. She lives in Dublin.

Jim Fitzpatrick, born in Dublin, is a self-taught artist. He is known worldwide for his artistic interpretations of Celtic mythology and, in particular, for his Thin Lizzy and Sinead O'Connor album covers and his iconic two-tone portrait of Che Guevara. He lives in Dublin.

Carlo Gébler was born in Dublin and brought up in London; he now lives outside Enniskillen. He is the author of novels, children's books, travel books and the memoir *Father & I*. He is currently writer in residence in HMP Maghaberry and Royal Literary Fund Fellow at Queen's University Belfast.

Hugo Hamilton is author of *The Speckled People*, the best-selling memoir of his unique German-Irish childhood in Dublin, which has been widely acclaimed as a classic and has been translated into fifteen languages. His latest novel, *Disguise*, continues to explore the central theme of belonging through the eyes of a changeling found at the end of the Second World War. He lives in Dublin.

Dermot Healy was born in County Westmeath. His novels are *Fighting with Shadows*, *The Goat's Song* and *Sudden Times*. He has also published several plays, collections of poetry and short stories, and his autobiography, *The Bend for Home*. A recipient of many literary awards, he lives in County Sligo.

Seamus Heaney was born in Derry. His bibliography is vast, his work encompassing poetry, criticism, theatre and translation. He was awarded the Nobel Prize for Literature in 1995. He lives in Dublin.

Ann Marie Hourihane is a journalist, author and sometime television presenter who lives in Dublin. Her book on Ireland's new-found prosperity *She Moves Through the Boom* was published way back in 2001. Her forthcoming book is entitled *Seasons of Devotion: Knock and the Making of Modern Ireland*. She has worked for several Irish newspapers and is currently a columnist for the *Irish Times*.

Tom Humphries was born in London, but grew up, and lives, in Dublin. A sportswriter and columnist, he has published six books, including *Laptop Dancing and the Nanny Goat Mambo: A Sports Writer's Year* and *Booked! (V. Carefully) Selected Writings*, a selection of his columns with the *Irish Times* and *Sports Illustrated* – all royalties from which he gave to Amnesty International.

Jennifer Johnston was born in Dublin. A novelist and playwright, she has received many awards. Her novels, including *The Captains and the Kings*, *How Many Miles to Babylon*, *Shadows on our Skin* and *The Invisible Worm*, have been published in many languages. She lives in Derry.

Neil Jordan was born in County Sligo. He has published one book of short stories, *A Night in Tunisia*, and four novels: *The Past*, *The Dream of a Beast*, *Sunrise and Seamonster*, and *Shade*. He has also scripted and directed several films, winning an Oscar for best original screenplay for *The Crying Game*. He lives in County Dublin.

Claire Kilroy is the author of three novels which loosely form a trilogy about the obsessions and exhilarations of art. Her debut, *All Summer*, was awarded the 2004 Rooney Prize for Irish Literature. Her second, *Tenderwire*, was shortlisted for the 2007 Irish Novel of the Year and the Kerry Group Irish Fiction Award. *All Names Have Been Changed*, her third novel, was published in 2009. She lives in Dublin.

Louis le Brocquy, born in 1916, lives in Dublin. A master of painting, illustration, printmaking, tapestry design and set design, his work is represented in the collections of numerous museums and galleries around the world. He has received widespread international acclaim during a career spanning over seventy years. His mother Sybil was co-founder of Amnesty International (Ireland) in 1962.

Brian Maguire was born in Dublin. He has always focused his art on the oppressed individual, perhaps best illustrated by his work in prisons and with street children. He exhibits widely throughout Europe, Japan and the Americas, and his work is represented in many international collections. He is Professor of Fine Art at the National College of Art and Design, in Dublin.

Alice Maher is a visual artist. She works in many different media including painting, drawing, sculpture, print, photography, installation and animation. She has exhibited widely throughout Ireland, Europe and the United States. She represented Ireland at the 22nd Sao Paolo Biennale. She lives and works in Dublin and Mayo.

Lara Marlowe is Washington correspondent for the *Irish Times*. As Paris correspondent from 1996 until 2009, she made frequent reporting trips to the Middle East. Marlowe has covered nearly all the major conflicts of the past quarter-century, including the Contra war in Nicaragua, the Lebanese and Algerian civil wars, the break-up of Yugoslavia, the Israeli-Palestinian conflict and the US invasion of Iraq.

Eugene McCabe was born in Glasgow in 1930 but has spent most of his life (seventy years) in Ireland. For four decades he farmed near Clones on the Monaghan/Fermanagh border, where he still lives. Married with four children, he is a playwright, short-story writer, novelist and occasional poet. Awards: Irish, English, European, Canadian and, most recently, American.

Colum McCann was born in Dublin. He is the author of two story collections and five novels, most recently *Let the Great World Spin*. He has received numerous international literary awards, and his short film *Everything in This Country Must* was nominated for an Oscar in 2005. He lives in New York with his wife and children, and teaches the Creative Writing MFA at Hunter College.

Frank McCourt was born, and lived his adult life, in New York – but spent much of his childhood in Limerick. His books include *Angela's Ashes* (which won the 1997 Pulitzer Prize), *'Tis, Teacher Man* and *Angela and The Baby Jesus*. He died in July 2009.

Nick Miller was born in London in 1962 and moved to Ireland in 1984. He now lives and works in County Sligo, and was elected to Aosdána in 2001. Major exhibitions include the New York Studio School (2008); Centre Culturel Irlandais, Paris (2007); Limerick City Gallery (2008); the Butler Gallery (2004); the Royal Hibernian Academy (2003); and the Irish Museum of Modern Art (1994).

Lia Mills is the author of two novels, *Another Alice* and *Nothing Simple*, and a memoir, *In Your Face*, which tells the story of a diagnosis of oral cancer and its treatment. She also writes short stories and literary non-fiction. She has worked on several public-art commissions, most recently *You Had To Be There!* and *Wake*, both for Ballymun Regeneration Ltd. Currently working on her third novel, she lives in Dublin.

Gary Mitchell was born in Belfast. An award-winning dramatist, his plays include *In a Little World of Our Own, As the Beast Sleeps, Sinking, Trust, The Force of Change, Tearing the Loom* and *Remnants of Fear*.

Eilís Ní Dhuibhne was born, and lives, in Dublin. She is a novelist, short-story writer, playwright and critic whose work has received many literary awards and is widely translated. She has worked as a librarian in the National Library and teacher of creative writing in Trinity College and UCD, and is a member of Aosdána.

Ross O'Carroll-Kelly: sportsman, boulevardier, lover of beautiful women and cad. Regularly described as the greatest Irish rugby player to never actually make it, he scored nine points in the Leinster Schools Senior Cup final of 1999 – nine more than he managed in the Leaving Cert. He has never worked a day in his life, has two children and is very happily separated. He's still a looker as well.

Joseph O'Connor was born in Dublin and is the author of six novels: *Cowboys and Indians, Desperadoes, The Salesman, Inishowen, Star of the Sea* and *Redemption Falls*.

Mick O'Dea, born in County Clare, is a visual artist. He works in pastel, acrylic and oil, a natural observer with an essentially humanistic approach; firm in the academic tradition, but not in the classical sense. He has exhibited widely throughout Ireland, Europe and the US. He lives in Dublin.

Mark O'Halloran is from County Clare. A scriptwriter and actor, he has written award-winning screenplays for the films *Adam and Paul* (in which he also co-starred) and *Garage*, and for the television series *Prosperity*. He lives in Dublin.

Glenn Patterson was born, and lives, in Belfast. He is the author of seven novels: *Burning Your Own*, *Fat Lad*, *Black Night at Big Thunder Mountain*, *The International*, *Number 5*, *That Which Was* and *The Third Party*. His non-fiction works are *Lapsed Protestant* and *Once Upon a Hill: Love in Troubled Times*.

Vivienne Roche RHA is a member of Aosdána. In 2009 she completed 'Bray Hare', a large-scale sculpture in steel, glass and light for Wicklow County Council. Other recent public commissions include 'Light Ensemble' for the new CIT Cork School of Music (2007–2008), 'NC Iris' in Dublin Docklands (2003–2006) and 'Whitelight Garden', a two-acre sculpture in Parkwest, Dublin (2000–2006). She is based in Garrettstown, County Cork.

Amelia Stein was born, and lives, in Dublin. She is the first photographer to be elected to the RHA and the first woman photographer to Aosdána. Working principally in black and white, many of her images have had worldwide exposure. Amelia's work is characterised by meticulous attention to detail in tandem with the attributes of traditional archival processes from portraiture to personal themes which include her relationship with aspects of the Irish landscape.

Gerard Stembridge was born in Limerick. A graduate of UCD, he lives in Dublin. He has written and directed film, theatre, television and radio. His latest work is a novel, *Counting Down*.

Colm Tóibín was born in County Wexford. His novels include *The South*, *The Heather Blazing*, *The Story of the Night*, *The Blackwater Lightship*, *The Master* and *Brooklyn*. His stories are collected as *Mothers and Sons*. His non-fiction includes *Bad Blood* and *The Sign of the Cross: Travels in Catholic Europe*. He lives in Dublin.

Irvine Welsh was born in Edinburgh. He has published seven novels, including *Trainspotting* and *Crime*. He has also published four collections of short stories, including, in 2009, *Reheated Cabbage*. He has written several plays and film scripts, and directed a number of short films. He is based in Dublin.